Progressions for Athlete and Coach Development

USA Swimming

ISBN: 0-7360-0181-6

Publication developed by Human Kinetics for USA Swimming.

All photos courtesy of USA Swimming.

Printed in Hong Kong 10 9 8 7 6 5 4 3 2 1

To contact USA Swimming:

USA Swimming
One Olympic Plaza
Colorado Springs, CO 80909
(719) 578-4578
(719) 578-4669 fax

contents

Introduction

Progressions for Athlete and Coach Development is a unique book! It is the first attempt by USA Swimming to acknowledge and plan for the development of the athlete as a whole person—physically, emotionally, mentally, and socially.

Progressions for Athlete Development

Part I, Progressions for Athlete Development, is a tool for coaches to use when designing the overall plan for an athlete's career development. The USA Swimming Technical Staff started to look at the career development process by trying to answer this question, "What is the best way to develop an athlete?" We have produced this book based on a great deal of discussion and the input from numerous USA Swimming technical committees and the Local Swim Committee (LSC) coaches' representatives.

The progressions comprise eight levels of development, which encompass six critical areas to help a coach guide this important journey for each and every athlete. The six areas are training, competitive performance, biomechanics, physiology, psychology, and character development and life skills.

As you read through the progressions, you may have some specific questions about the development of your particular athletes. The progressions are meant to be a tool or a yardstick to evaluate the overall development and progress of your swimmers. The "how" of getting your athletes to each milestone is completely up to you. Helping your athletes reach these accomplishments will be the true result of balancing the art and science of coaching.

Progressions for Athlete and Coach Development is by no means meant to create clone coaching! Will every athlete progress to level 8? No. Will every athlete excel at the same pace? No. Can an athlete make it to the upper levels by virtue of his or her talent and achievements? Only in the categories of training parameters and competitive performance. The athlete could be at level 4 in character development for his or her entire life. In other cases, just the opposite is true. We have all coached kids who are head and shoulders above anyone when it comes to life skills such as making a commitment and having a work ethic, but unfortunately some of these athletes will never make a junior championship cut. These athletes may be level 8 in the character development category, but they may never achieve higher than level 4 or 5 in the competitive performance area. We hope that the progressions will help you address the full development of each one of your swimmers.

We thank all of the coaches and experts who sent us their constructive comments. In particular, we would like to thank Dr. Alan Goldberg for his contributions to the psychological area and Bob Staab for his contributions to the training and character development and life skills area.

Although we view this book as a "work in progress," it is now time for these progressions to be used by coaches. With time, the progressions will become a reflection of the true developmental process each swimmer goes through, a process that recognizes that every swimmer who enters our sport begins a journey with his or her own road map. Each swimmer's journey proceeds at an individual pace, with many different levels of success. We hope you find these progressions helpful in creating a career plan for the development of your swimmers. USA Swimming would appreciate it if you would provide us with feedback that will continue to shape and improve this book. Please send your ideas and suggestions about part I to the Athlete Services Director, USA Swimming, One Olympic Plaza, Colorado Springs, CO, 80909.

Progressions for Coach Development

As a companion piece to the Progressions for Athlete Development, part II, Progressions for Coach Development, provides general concepts to the coach about how to accomplish development in five of the six areas listed in part I. (We did not include the "competitive performance" category because competitive performance is an outcome of the other five areas.) One coach described the Progressions for Coach Development as the "Cliff notes" of coaching. Where possible, an attempt has been made to link specific components of skill development in the Progressions for Coach Development with a level from the Progressions for Athlete Development. This is identified in parentheses following a skill or concept (e.g., "level 5" would refer to a skill listed in level 5 in the Progressions for Athlete Development).

Each chapter in part II was written to augment the Progressions for Athlete Development areas by providing both theoretical and practical information. Chapter 3, Training, provides the basics for set design. Physiology, chapter 5, contains more in-depth theoretical information that supports the training information given in chapter 3. Chapters 4, 6, and 7, Biomechanics, Character Development and Life Skills, and Psychology, provide a stepwise approach to accomplish the levels assigned in the Progressions for Athlete Development.

Some chapters of the Progressions for Coach Development are very technical in nature and are not necessarily meant to be used or understood by a first-time or entry-level coach. Please remember that this manual is offered to provide general guidelines on material for a coach to help an athlete reach all the levels described in the Progressions for Athlete Development. As a swimmer progresses up the levels in the Progressions for Athlete Development, the higher levels involve much more technical coaching issues than do the lower levels. This is especially true for a coach who works with an athlete who is in level 8, which means that the athlete is on the World Championship or Olympic Team.

We also have incorporated the USA Swimming *Training Categories Handbook* into the appendixes of this document. Appendix A is the general description of concepts underlying training categories. Appendix B gives examples of different ways a coach might try to determine training paces to train specific energy systems. We would like to thank Dr. Rick Sharp for his contributions of appendix B.

If you have any ideas or suggestions on the Progressions for Athlete and Coach Development, please feel free to send them to the Coach Services Director, USA Swimming, One Olympic Plaza, Colorado Springs, CO, 80909.

We hope that you find both the Progressions for Athlete Development and the Progressions for Coach Development helpful in creating a career plan for the development of your swimmers.

USA Swimming
Sport Development Division

Part I

Progressions for Athlete Development

The Progressions for Athlete Development are divided into two sections. Chapter 1 explains the areas of development and lists the requirements for the prerequisite level through level 8. This format allows you to see how the particular area grows and builds from beginning to end. Read the introduction to each section and then review the skills at each level to get an idea of how the progressions flow.

Chapter 2 shows each level, starting with the prerequisites and ending with level 8, and the requirements for the six main categories. The chapter explains how all of the categories progress as the athlete moves from one level to the next.

Please be aware that all of the progressions are exit criteria—that is, the athlete moves to the next level only after he or she has successfully completed the skill(s) at the prior level.

Swimmers are multidimensional and develop at different rates; sometimes they excel in some areas faster than in others. In looking at the six areas of development—training requirements, competitive performance, biomechanical progressions, physiological progressions, character development and life skills, and psychological skills—you may find that your swimmers are working in levels that look like those represented in the chart below.

You may decide to place your swimmers in training groups based on these progressions and to focus your educational sessions based on the swimmers' cognitive skills.

	Swimmer A	Swimmer B
Training requirements	5	3
Competitive performance	5	2
Biomechanical progressions	4	3
Physiological progressions	3	3
Character development and life skills	6	4
Psychological skills	2	5

How to Use Progressions for Athlete Development

The Progressions for Athlete Development are designed to be used as a tool by the professional coach. Professional, in this case, does not refer to whether you are full or part time but rather to how you approach your coaching. The progressions can be used to enhance your coaching by giving specific examples of what an athlete may need to accomplish at different levels to reach his or her potential. If you feel uncomfortable addressing a particular area, you may want to consider bringing in an expert presenter, or better yet, attending a coaches' education program that features the area in which you require greater expertise. By educating yourself, you will be better prepared to address all areas of the progressions described in this book.

Listed next are examples of how the Progressions for Athlete Development can be used:

❖ Take a topic from an area of development, and hold a series of team meetings around that topic. These meetings may be given for athletes and/or their parents. For example, here are some meeting topics taken from the psychological skills category:

Meeting One	Self-talk
Meeting Two	Concentration
Meeting Three	Visualization
Meeting Four	Goal setting

❖ The progressions can serve as the basis for a club award system. Give special recognition to a swimmer who moves to the next level. Post a chart that allows swimmers to mark down when they have completed a specific skill or task.

❖ Focus on the career development of an athlete, so that his or her long-term development is emphasized.

❖ Emphasize the six different areas of development so that the swimmer must think about more than just swimming fast. This multidimensional focus helps develop a well-rounded athlete.

❖ Teach swimmers different aspects of the biomechanical and physiological areas to get them to also focus on technique, stroke count, distance per stroke, heart rate, etc.

❖ This book may be used to construct progressions that are in line with your present team structure. A beginning team may have as their top athletes swimmers with level 4 competitive performances, some athletes with level 3 training requirements, and the remainder with a variety of skill levels in the other areas. A coach may decide to develop progressions for his or her athletes and adopt them as follows:

1. Level 5 could become a level 8 for a particular team.
2. Each level below level 5 could be broken down into smaller steps so the athletes see their progress and feel that they are moving up the ladder of success.
3. Athletes could be divided into training groups to work on specific increments of the training requirements listed.
4. Outside training could take place that teaches many of the cognitive skills of swimming.
5. Progress charts (using simple grid charts available at teacher supply stores) could be posted showing each swimmer's progress.
6. Athletes could develop their own checklists of skills accomplished.
7. Weekly or monthly "graduation ceremonies" could be held as athletes fulfill requirements at different levels.
8. As the team grows and individual athletes progress, new challenges, based on this model, could be implemented.

Key Terms

The section that follows provide terms and their basic definitions that will be helpful in understanding the Progressions for Athlete Development that follow in chapters 1 and 2. First the coach should understand these terms. The coach can then, in turn, instruct the athlete.

"Act as if" strategy—This is a coping strategy. When an athlete is in an uncomfortable or nervous situation, the athlete would act as if he or she is not nervous. Acting calm and confident actually soothes the physiological changes that occur when one is nervous. Breathing and heart rate slow down, and this in turn causes the muscles to relax.

Anabolic agents—Prohibited substances that increase protein synthesis, which may, with training and proper nutrition, create an increase in lean muscle mass.

Arousal control techniques—Four techniques athletes can use to control arousal level include deep breathing (belly breathing), progressive muscle relaxation, positive self-talk, and the "act as if" strategy.

Arousal level—Arousal can be best understood as having both a somatic (physical) and a cognitive (mental) component. This means that arousal has a physical effect on the athlete such as increased heart rate, increased muscle activation, increased sweating, high adrenaline, and so on. Arousal also has an effect on the athlete's cognitive functioning (self-talk, concentration, images).

Cognitive skills—The swimmer is able to demonstrate knowledge through thought processes. For example, during a set a coach asks a group of eight-year-olds to count five stroke cycles from a freestyle push-off, stop, and stand up and look at the coach. The swimmers do this skill 10 times, demonstrating the cognitive skill of counting five complete stroke cycles.

Computing stroke rate and distance per stroke—Here is one method (see p. 61 for more information):

1. Using a stopwatch, time the swimmer for four complete stroke cycles. A sample time might be 4.68 seconds.
2. Divide 60 seconds by the time (4.68 seconds) and then multiply by the number of stroke cycles (60 divided by 4.68 equals 12.82 times 4 stroke cycles equals 51.2 cycles per minute). The swimmer has a stroke rate of 51.2 cycles per minute and is traveling a distance of 0.85 meters for each complete stroke cycle.
3. Distance per stroke is calculated by dividing the swimming speed by the cycles per second (e.g., 1.44 meters per second divided by 0.85 cycles per second equals 1.69 meters per cycle).

CP system—The metabolic pathway that uses creatine phosphate (CP) as a fuel. Creatine phosphate is stored in the muscle and provides a rapid, short-term energy source.

Diaphragmatic breathing—Commonly referred to as "belly" breathing. The swimmer concentrates on the navel rising on the inhalation instead of the shoulders and upper body.

Distance per stroke—How far a swimmer moves forward in one complete stroke cycle.

Diuretics—Prohibited substances that eliminate excess fluid from body tissue in certain pathological conditions and manage high blood pressure.

Exit criteria—Skills or knowledge within a progression area that the athlete should demonstrate successfully before moving on to the next level. Exit criteria might be in the form of physical ability or demonstrated knowledge.

Individual Medley (IM)—A competitive event where the athlete swims one quarter of the prescribed distance using each of the following strokes in this order: butterfly, backstroke, breaststroke, and freestyle.

Individual zones of optimal functioning (IZOF)—This term refers to the fact that each athlete has a level, or zone of arousal, at which they tend to perform best. It is up to the individual athletes to determine if they need a high, low, or medium arousal level to perform at their best.

Lactate tolerance sets—A training method designed to subject the swimmer to high levels of lactic acid in the blood.

Long course meters (LCM)—50-meter pools, where one length of the pool is equal to 50 meters.

Narcotics—Prohibited substances that function as pain killers, produce sensations of euphoria or psychological stimulation, false feelings of invincibility, and illusions of athletic prowess beyond the swimmer's inherent ability.

Peptide and glycoprotein hormones and analogues—Prohibited substances that lead to an increased rate of production of endogenous androgenic steroids and increase the blood levels of endogenous corticosteroids.

Physical skill—Demonstrated physical mastery of a skill. For example, a swimmer might be asked to demonstrate his or her physical skill by performing a legal 200 individual medley. The swimmer, either in practice or a meet, is able to demonstrate the correct and legal stroke technique for a 200 IM, including all four strokes and turns associated with that swim.

Prone position—Position of a swimmer in relation to the bottom of the pool, where the swimmer is on his or her stomach or face down.

Recommended daily allowance (RDA)—The daily intake level of nutrients that the USDA recommends for average citizens.

Self-talk—One's inner voice, through which one gives oneself either positive or negative messages. Athletes who spend time training their self-talk to be positive have better self-control and self-confidence.

Short-course yards (SCY)—25-yard pools, where one length of the pool is equal to 25 yards.

Stimulants—Prohibited substances that increase alertness, reduce fatigue, and may increase competitiveness and hostility.

Streamlining—To position the body in a manner that reduces the resistance from the water. Streamlining should be applied during a start and push-off from the wall by using a tight "torpedo" position.

Stroke cycle—A complete stroke cycle is measured consistently by the coach. Usually, as in freestyle and backstroke, a complete stroke cycle is measured from the time the fingertips enter the water on one hand until the fingertips enter the water again on the same hand. A complete butterfly stroke cycle is measured from the time both hands enter the water until they enter it again. Breaststroke stroke cycles are usually measured after the start or the pullout and can be measured either when the coach sees the hands at full extension or the head going underwater. The key is that measurements be taken consistently.

Stroke rate—An indicator of how fast a swimmer is moving his or her body through the water. Stroke rate may be measured as the amount of time it takes a swimmer to complete two, three, or four complete stroke cycles. It is usually expressed in cycles per minute or cycles per second.

Supine position—Position of a swimmer in relation to the bottom of the pool where the swimmer is on his or her back or face up.

Swimming speed—Is measured as velocity and in most swimming research is noted as meters per second. To calculate swimming speed, divide the distance covered by the time. For example, a swimmer completes a 50-meter freestyle swim in 34.5 seconds; 50 divided by 34.5 seconds equals 1.44 meters per second.

T30—An endurance swim in which the swimmer maintains the fastest average possible for a period of 30 minutes, and the coach records the distance completed to get an average pace per 100 yards or meters. This average pace can then be used as the basis for future training paces. This can also be a 3,000 swim for time also getting an average pace per 100 yards or meters. For younger swimmers or athletes swimming a stroke other than freestyle, a T20 or 20-minute swim can be used.

Training periodization—A type of training where the type and amount of training are broken up into sections or periods. The training periods can last days or years.

Uncontrollables—Things that are outside of the athlete's personal control—for example, how fast your competitor will swim, in what lane you will swim, the weather, and so on.

Ways to minimize drag in the water—Drag forces act opposite to the direction a swimmer is moving. Ways to minimize the effects of drag are to increase the propulsive force by efficient technique or minimize the resistive forces. Resistive forces are factors such as the total surface area (the more streamlined a swimmer is in pushing off the walls, the less total surface area, or frontal resistance, that must be overcome) or the form drag (the less hip sway a swimmer has, the less body movement the swimmer uses against the water).

one

Areas of Development

This chapter is in chart form. Each chart illustrates one of the six areas of development and lists the requirements for the prerequisite level through level 8. This format allows you to see how the particular area builds from beginning to end.

Training

The workout sets listed in the training category are not intended to represent a full menu of sets for each of the energy systems. The critically important lactate tolerance sets and other anaerobic sets are not included because swimmers at any level can "keep up" with the long rest intervals. The intervals that are presented in the training category of this book represent the minimum pace that the swimmers must be able to sustain to handle the aerobic work in the next level. Needless to say, both the intervals and the length of the aerobic sets at any given level will vary throughout the season. As is the case with all of the other information presented in the book, coaches may need to modify these guidelines to suit the particular needs of their athletes and programs.

Prerequisite

Physical
Swims 25 yards/meters in the prone or supine position from a push-off.

Level 1

Physical

1. Swims 25 yards/meters of freestyle and backstroke.
2. Starts and finishes at the wall.

Cognitive
Begins to use the pace clock.

Level 2

Physical
Can complete the following practice sets:

6 × 50 Free
6 × 50 Back
6 × 50 Breast
6 × 50 Fly
6 × 50 Kick

Cognitive
Accurately counts and computes distances.

Level 3

Physical
Can complete the following practice sets:

	LCM	SCY
Ages 10 and under		
3 × 200 IM on	4:20	3:50
6 × 100 Kick on	2:20	2:10
8 × 100 Free on	2:00	1:50
And any one of the following sets:		
12 × 100 Free on	1:55	1:45
6 × 100 Fly on	2:20	2:10
12 × 100 Back on	2:10	2:00
12 × 100 Breast on	2:20	2:10
Ages 11-12		
4 × 200 IM on	4:10	3:45
7 × 100 Kick on	2:20	2:10
10 × 100 Free on	1:50	1:40
And any one of the following sets:		
16 × 100 Free on	1:45	1:35
9 × 100 Fly on	2:10	2:00
16 × 100 Back on	2:00	1:50
16 × 100 Breast on	2:10	2:00
Ages 13 and over		
6 × 200 IM on	4:00	3:40
8 × 100 Kick on	2:20	2:10
12 × 100 Free on	1:45	1:35
And any one of the following sets:		
16 × 100 Free on	1:35	1:25
12 × 100 Fly on	2:00	1:50
16 × 100 Back on	1:50	1:40
16 × 100 Breast on	2:00	1:50

Level 4

Physical
Can complete the following practice sets:

	LCM	SCY
6 × 200 IM on	3:40	3:20
8 × 100 Kick on	2:10	2:00
16 × 100 Free on	1:40	1:30
And any one of the following sets:		
20 × 100 Free on	1:30	1:20
20 × 100 Back on	1:40	1:30
20 × 100 Breast on	1:50	1:40
20 × 100 Fly on	1:40	1:30

Training

Level 5

Physical

Can complete the following practice sets:

	LCM	SCY
4 × 400 IM on	6:40	6:00
12 × 100 Kick on	2:00	1:50
24 × 100 Free on	1:30	1:20

And any one of the following sets:

	LCM	SCY
24 × 100 Free on	1:20	1:10
24 × 100 Back on	1:30	1:20
24 × 100 Breast on	1:40	1:30
24 × 100 Fly on	1:30	1:20

Level 6

Physical

Can complete the following practice sets:

	LCM
4 × 400 IM on	6:20
12 × 100 Kick on	1:55
24 × 100 Free on	1:25

And any one of the following:

	LCM
24 × 100 Free on	1:15
24 × 100 Back on	1:25
24 × 100 Breast on	1:35
24 × 100 Fly on	1:25

Level 7

Physical

Can complete the following practice sets:

	LCM
4 × 400 IM on	6:00
12 × 100 Kick on	1:50
24 × 100 Free on	1:20

And any one of the following:

	LCM
24 × 100 Free on	1:12 (Women) 1:08 (Men)
24 × 100 Back on	1:20 (Women) 1:15 (Men)
24 × 100 Breast on	1:30 (Women) 1:25 (Men)
24 × 100 Fly on	1:20 (Women) 1:15 (Men)

Level 8

Physical

Can complete the following practice sets:

	LCM
4 × 400 IM on	5:40
12 × 100 Kick on	1:45
24 × 100 Free on	1:15

Competitive Performance

The competitive performance section is designed to allow the coach to establish a progression of times for the athlete to achieve in competition before the athlete can move to the next level. The focus is very light in the first three levels, which include the prerequisite level; performance times are introduced in level three. One of the goals in this category is to prepare the athlete for long-term development by emphasizing all four strokes, avoiding specialization until later in the athlete's career.

The competitive time progressions are designed to dovetail into what is expected in practice performances. The times listed next for each level are used to determine the training speeds in the training category.

Prerequisite

None

Level 1

None

Level 2

Has participated in competitive situations for the primary purpose of skill development (i.e., time trials, intrasquad meets, dual meets, and other entry-level competitions).

Level 3

Has competed in all the events offered in his or her age group and has met all of the following time standards (in yards or meters) in a sanctioned USA Swimming Meet.

	LCM	SCY
100 Free	1:20	1:10
100 Back	1:35	1:25
100 Breast	1:50	1:35
100 Fly	1:40	1:25
200 IM	3:20	2:55

Level 4

Has competed in all the events offered in his or her age group and has met all of the following time standards (in yards or meters) in a Sanctioned USA Swimming Meet.

	LCM	SCY
100 Free	1:15	1:05
200 Free	2:40	2:20
400/500 Free	5:20	6:00
800/1000 Free	10:40	12:00
1500/1650 Free	20:00	19:45
100 Back	1:25	1:15
100 Breast	1:35	1:25
100 Fly	1:25	1:15
200 IM	3:00	2:40

Competitive Performance

Level 5

Must achieve at least one time standard from the Age Group Time Standards, Championship Based Standards, level 1. (See current *USA Swimming Rules & Regulations* for time standards, or check the USA Swimming web page at http://www.usa-swimming.org/.)

Level 6

Has attained a Junior Championship Time Standard in one or more individual events. (See current *USA Swimming Rules & Regulations* for time standards, or check the USA Swimming web page at http://www.usa-swimming.org/.)

Level 7

Has attained a National Championship Time Standard in one or more individual events. (See current *USA Swimming Rules & Regulations* for time standards, or check the USA Swimming web page at http://www.usa-swimming.org/.)

Level 8

Ranked among the Top 8 fastest swimmers in the world or is a member of the USA Olympic Team.

Biomechanics

The biomechanical progressions emphasize technique acquisition in the development of swimmers. The goal here is not to dictate how technique should be taught but to provide a step-by-step developmental time line to keep athletes advancing throughout their careers.

The levels focus on both creation of propulsion through sculling and the minimization of water drag during training and races. Both factors are critical in improving overall swimming speed.

The distance per stroke cycle (one complete cycle, e.g., right-arm entry to right-arm entry in freestyle and backstroke) is very important to proper biomechanics and must be reinforced as the swimmer progresses through the developmental levels. Research continually shows that long distance per stroke is the most important factor in elite level swimming. Monitoring an athlete's distance per stroke cycle is the simplest, most objective tool that can be used in the field to assess biomechanical technique. Distance per stroke cycle should lengthen as technique improves.

Prerequisites

1. Float face down for a period of one minute. (Swimmers may breathe when necessary but may not touch the bottom of the pool.)
2. Float face up with little or no movement for a period of one minute without touching the bottom of the pool.
3. From a standing position, or holding on to the side of the pool, demonstrate rhythmic breathing, exhaling underwater and inhaling above water.

Level 1

Physical

1. From a push maintain a prone streamlined body position, defined as one hand on top of the other, ears between the upper arms, lower body stretched long, and toes pointed.
2. Hold this position for at least one and one-half body lengths, and be able to vary the depth of the underwater push-off.
3. Execute a breakout from a push by holding the streamlined position; then initiate a kicking action and progress to the surface of the water with a pull to the surface.
4. Propel forward in a prone position for at least one length of the pool.
5. Propel forward in a supine position for at least one length of the pool.
6. Maintain a vertical, stationary position with little or no leg movement in deep water, using a sculling motion.
7. Stroke progressions: Complete progressions for freestyle and backstroke. Begin to develop the butterfly and breaststroke.

Freestyle

a. Complete the legal freestyle technique using arms and legs for one length of the pool.
b. Demonstrate shoulder and hip rolling motion during the freestyle stroke.
c. Demonstrate the ability to comfortably take a breath on either the right or left side.

Backstroke

a. Complete the legal backstroke technique using arms and legs for one length of the pool.
b. Demonstrate shoulder and hip rolling motion during the backstroke.

8. Demonstrate proper dive from the side of the pool with a streamlined glide to the surface (follow the guidelines in the American Red Cross publication, *Safety Training for Swim Coaches*).
9. Perform an open turn, either prone or supine, where the hand touches the wall first, the body rotates to place the feet against the wall, the body drops underwater, and the swimmer pushes off in a streamlined position.

Cognitive

1. The swimmer knows which letter of the alphabet best describes the freestyle pulling pattern.
2. The swimmer can count up to five complete stroke cycles of freestyle.
3. The swimmer can count up to five complete stroke cycles of backstroke.

Level 2

Physical

1. Execute a start from the blocks. Hold the underwater streamlined position for one and one-half body lengths, initiate a kicking action for one body length, and progress to the surface of the water with a pull.
2. Execute a legal freestyle, backstroke, butterfly, and breaststroke turn, including an approach of at least 10 yards/meters.
3. Stroke progression: Complete progressions for the butterfly and breaststroke.

Butterfly

a. Complete one length of the pool with legal butterfly form.
b. Demonstrate correct timing of the pull, kick, and breath during the butterfly.
c. Demonstrate an undulating motion during the butterfly stroke.

Breaststroke

a. Complete one length of the pool with legal breaststroke form.
b. Demonstrate correct timing of the pull, kick, and breath during the breaststroke.

4. Perform 100 yards or 100 meters of individual medley with legal technique.

Cognitive

1. From a push the swimmer counts the number of stroke cycles of freestyle, and the coach records the time for one length of the pool.
2. From a push the swimmer counts the number of stroke cycles of backstroke, and the coach records the time for one length of the pool.
3. From a push the swimmer counts the number of stroke cycles of butterfly, and the coach records the time for one length of the pool.
4. From a push the swimmer counts the number of stroke cycles of breaststroke, and the coach records the time for one length of the pool.

Biomechanics

Level 3

Physical

Perform a legal 200 individual medley swim.

Cognitive

1. Complete one length of freestyle holding the same time or faster but using at least one less stroke cycle than in level 2.
2. Complete one length of backstroke holding the same time or faster but using at least one less stroke cycle than in level 2.
3. Complete one length of butterfly holding the same time or faster but using at least one less stroke cycle than in level 2.
4. Complete one length of breaststroke holding the same time or faster but using at least one less stroke cycle than in level 2.

Level 4

Physical

1. Complete one length of each stroke holding the same time or faster but using fewer stroke cycles than in level 3.
2. Maintain consistent stroke rates and times in training sets.

Cognitive

1. The swimmer understands the relationship between distance per stroke, stroke rate, and swimming speed.
2. The swimmer can name two ways to minimize resistance or drag from the water.
3. The swimmer can explain one reason why sculling is important in creating propulsion.

Level 5

Physical

Perform a 400 individual medley swim with correct transitions between strokes.

Cognitive

The swimmer, with the assistance of his or her coach, can calculate swimming speed, distance per stroke, and stroke rate during competition and training.

Level 6

Physical

1. Continue to decrease the number of stroke cycles, or swim faster with the same number of cycles.
2. Decrease the number of cycles per length during competition.

Cognitive

The swimmer can calculate swimming speed, distance per stroke, and stroke rate.

Level 7

Physical

Continue to improve distance per stroke and/or swimming speed during competition and training.

Level 8

Physical

Continue to improve distance per stroke and/or swimming speed during competition and training.

Physiology

A variety of physiological adaptations are required for optimal performance because events in competitive swimming range in duration from about 20 seconds up to a little less than 20 minutes. Elements of both speed and endurance have been shown to be important factors in competitive success. Thus, competitive swimmers spend a great deal of their training efforts on enhancing their physiological capacities to optimize their sprint and endurance abilities. The development of physiological systems for success must coincide with the athlete's responsiveness to the various forms of conditioning at different times during his or her growth and development. For example, it has been shown that children have a limited capacity to perform and adapt to high-intensity anaerobic work prior to puberty. Thus, a well-planned training program designed to maximize the swimmers' ultimate performance potential will avoid placing too much emphasis on this kind of physiological conditioning until the late adolescent phase of development. Instead, the focus in early childhood should be on developing the skills and aerobic endurance necessary to perform the higher-intensity training later in the swimmers' careers. The physiological progressions included in this book were designed to reflect this philosophy by introducing physiological capacities at the appropriate times of the swimmer's career. In addition, field tests of physiological capacities are recommended instead of laboratory-based tests because of the lack of access to laboratory testing by most athletes and coaches. By taking this approach, we hope to provide guidance to our coaches and athletes and equip them with tools to evaluate the athletes' progress.

Prerequisite

None

Level 1

Physical

1. Coordinated movement patterns: swims freestyle and backstroke with legal form.
2. Aerobic endurance
   a. Can complete a 30-minute practice session.
   b. Can perform a continuous swim for five minutes.

Level 2

Physical

1. Coordinated movement patterns: swims all four strokes.
2. Aerobic endurance: can perform continuous swim for 10 minutes.

Cognitive

1. The swimmer begins to understand maturation, physical development, and nutrition.
   a. Understands and accepts individual differences in physical size within an age group.
   b. Understands that energy for exercise is derived from nutrition.

Level 3

Physical

1. Coordinated movement patterns: swims all four strokes with legal form.
2. Aerobic endurance: performs T30 or other threshold set one time per season.

Cognitive

1. Swimmer understands maturation and physical development: begins to understand relationship between training programs, maturation, and physical development.
2. Swimmer understands the purpose of heart rate measurement.
3. The swimmer can measure his or her own resting and exercise heart rate.
4. The swimmer understands the importance of muscular flexibility in swimming performance.

Level 4

Physical

Aerobic endurance: swims a T30 or other threshold set two times per season with improvement.

Cognitive

1. The swimmer understands the concept of a balanced diet and basic fuels used during swimming training.
2. The swimmer begins to understand the basics of different energy system usage in sprinting versus distance swimming.
3. The swimmer can use heart rate measurement to monitor exercise intensity and recovery.

Physiology

Level 5

Physical

1. Muscular strength and endurance: can perform sit-ups, push-ups, and pull-ups (chin-ups).
2. Aerobic endurance: swims a T30 or other threshold set three times per season with continuous improvement.
3. Sprint capacity/CP system: swims 12 × 25 (three butterfly, three backstroke, three breaststroke, and three freestyle) on 3:00 (three per stroke) at maximum velocity three times per season.

Cognitive

1. The swimmer understands energy systems: can explain aerobic and anaerobic systems of energy delivery.
2. The swimmer understands nutritional requirements of training and competition: demonstrates understanding of basic nutrition principles, fuels for swimming performance, training diets, hydration, RDAs for swimmers, and the importance of eating a balanced diet.
3. The swimmer demonstrates understanding of the relationship between training programs and maturation and development and their effects on competitive and training performance.
4. The swimmer understands how to use heart rate measurement to monitor training progress.

Level 6

Physical

1. Muscular strength and endurance: can perform sit-ups, push-ups, and pull-ups (chin-ups) with improvement from previous level.
2. Aerobic endurance: performs T30 or other threshold set three times per season with continuous improvement.
3. Lactate tolerance: performs a set of 12 × 100 (or until failure) on 2:30 holding current best 200 pace (2nd 100 split) three times per season with continuous improvement.
4. Sprint capacity/CP system: performs 12 × 25 on 3:00 (specialty stroke) at maximum velocity.

Cognitive

1. The swimmer demonstrates knowledge of energy systems.
   a. Can describe the relationship between training sets and energy systems.
   b. Demonstrates an understanding of training periodization.
2. The swimmer understands nutritional requirements of training and competition.

Level 7

Physical

1. Muscular strength and endurance: demonstrates improvement in muscular endurance (stroke specific).
2. Aerobic endurance: performs a T30 or other threshold set three times per season with continuous improvement.
3. Lactate tolerance: performs a set of 12 × 100 (or until failure) on 2:30 holding current best 200 pace (2nd 100 split) three times per season with continuous improvement.
4. Sprint capacity/CP system: performs 12 × 25 on 3:00 (specialty stroke) at maximum velocity three times per season with continuous improvement.

Cognitive

1. The swimmer demonstrates knowledge of energy systems.
   a. Demonstrates knowledge of personal training velocities for each training category.
   b. Can discuss training needs based on test-set results.
2. The swimmer develops and understands nutritional plan for training and competition.

Level 8

Physical

1. Muscular strength and endurance:
   a. Demonstrates maintenance of muscular strength.
   b. Demonstrates improvement in stroke-specific muscular endurance.
2. Aerobic endurance: performs a T30 or other threshold set three times per season with continuous improvement.
3. Lactate tolerance: demonstrates ability to perform a set of 12 × 100 (or until failure) on 2:30 holding current best 200 pace (2nd 100 split) three times per season with continuous improvement.
4. Sprint capacity/CP system: performs 12 × 25 on 3:00 (specialty stroke) at maximum velocity three times per season with continuous improvement.

Cognitive

The swimmer understands the nutritional requirements of training and competition; he or she demonstrates the ability to apply nutritional information to daily living.

Character Development and Life Skills

Many coaches support learning life skills as a major benefit of participating in a swim program. These skills include such things as championship behavior and accountability, work ethic and self-discipline, time management, and commitment and loyalty. Ten years after a swimmer has stopped swimming the items most often mentioned about his or her swimming career are in this category. In our review of swimming literature, however, we did not find much information regarding at what level of a swimmer's career these issues should be addressed. As in all the other categories presented, each level builds upon the previous level.

Prerequisite

None

Level 1

Championship Behavior and Accountability

1. The swimmer understands that he or she is part of a team and has respect for his or her teammates.
2. The swimmer listens to recommendations from the coach and tries to make the appropriate changes.
3. The swimmer understands appropriate team rules and the consequences of breaking the rules.

Work Ethic and Self-Discipline

1. The swimmer will pick up and put away any equipment he or she used in practice.
2. The swimmer will be ready to start practice on time with the appropriate equipment (suits, goggles, etc.).
3. The swimmer understands the importance of giving the coach his or her undivided attention while the coach is talking. The swimmer should focus his or her eyes on the coach and remain quiet when the coach is talking. The swimmer will also follow directions set forth by the coach in practice.
4. The swimmer will "Just say no!" to drugs and other harmful substances.
5. The swimmer will show respect for the facilities and equipment.

Time Management

The swimmer will arrive at practice sessions on time.

Commitment and Team Loyalty

1. The swimmer will know the team name and team colors.
2. The swimmer will know the names of teammates and coaches in his or her practice group.
3. The swimmer will know the name of any other training group(s) on the team besides his or her own group (e.g., age group 1, age group 2, senior, and national).

Level 2

Championship Behavior and Accountability

1. The swimmer demonstrates an understanding of sportsmanship–championship behavior (e.g., doesn't throw goggles, congratulates opponents).
2. The swimmer will treat teammates, parents, and coaches like he or she would want to be treated.
3. The swimmer talks to the coach before and after each race.

Work Ethic and Self-Discipline

1. During practice the swimmer will
   a. leave on time during sets,
   b. start and finish at the wall,
   c. swim the set in the prescribed manner (e.g., doesn't do freestyle on butterfly sets, doesn't pull on kicking sets, performs all turns legally), and
   d. swim the entire set (e.g., doesn't walk on bottom, counts accurately).
2. The swimmer will communicate with his or her coach.

Time Management

1. The swimmer understands the importance of hard work in the classroom and will complete his or her homework on time.
2. The swimmer will turn in appropriate team paperwork in a timely fashion (meet entries, release forms, change of address, etc.).

Commitment and Team Loyalty

1. The swimmer will learn the history of the team.
2. The swimmer chooses a swimming hero (may be a member of his or her team) and knows the event in which the individual competed or competes.
3. The swimmer takes pride in being a member of the team, which the swimmer demonstrates by
   a. participating in team cheers,
   b. knowing the coaches' names, and
   c. cheering on teammates during swims (practice or meets).

Level 3

Championship Behavior and Accountability

The swimmer will demonstrate a higher level of sportsmanship–championship behavior than in level 2 (e.g., respects competitors and gets along with friends regardless of ability level).

Work Ethic and Self-Discipline

1. The swimmer attends the recommended meets and understands the importance of being on time for meet warm-ups.
2. The swimmer will meet the established attendance requirements.
3. The swimmer will understand why he or she must "Just say no!" to drugs and other harmful substances.
4. The swimmer will learn to challenge him- or herself to perform to the utmost of his or her ability in practice.

Time Management

The swimmer demonstrates an ability to balance school and outside activities.

Commitment and Loyalty

The swimmer chooses a national swimming hero and knows the event in which he or she competed or competes.

Level 4

Championship Behavior and Accountability

The swimmer will know the names of competitors.

Work Ethic and Self-Discipline

1. The swimmer is not influenced by the negative behavior of his or her teammates.
2. The swimmer understands and takes responsibility for attendance, performance, and habits in practice and how these three relate to meet performance.

Character Development and Life Skills

Level 5

Championship Behavior and Accountability

The swimmer learns to accept responsibility for his or her performance.

Work Ethic and Self-Discipline

1. The swimmer will learn coping strategies to deal with peer pressure.
2. The swimmer will learn coping strategies to deal with parent pressure.
3. The swimmer will be able to list the five classes of prohibited substances.
4. The swimmer understands and performs personal race strategies.

Time Management

The swimmer demonstrates an ability to balance school, social activities, swimming, and family.

Commitment and Team Loyalty

1. The swimmer can effectively communicate his or her commitment to the swimmer's parents, coach, and teammates.
2. The swimmer knows the team goals and will take an active part in developing specific and attainable practice group goals.
3. The swimmer understands the relationship between his or her personal commitment level and results.

Level 6

Championship Behavior and Accountability

The swimmer accepts the responsibility of being a leader and/or role model. The swimmer will lead by being a positive example.

Work Ethic and Self-Discipline

1. The swimmer will be able to explain the rationale of the five categories of banned substances.
2. The swimmer will demonstrate an understanding of the short- and long-term effects of performance-enhancing drugs.

Time Management

The swimmer has mastered time management skills so outside activities do not interfere with practice and meet attendance.

Commitment and Team Loyalty

1. The swimmer understands the need to sacrifice self-interest for team goals.
2. The swimmer demonstrates commitment to his or her team by continued dedicated membership.

Level 7

Championship Behavior and Accountability

1. The swimmer demonstrates leadership responsibilities by working with younger swimmers (e.g., talking with them, water work).
2. The swimmer understands the importance of seasonal, yearly, and quadrennial planning and the consistency of the plan within each of the cycles.
3. The swimmer will recognize the effects of poor communication.

Work Ethic and Self-Discipline

1. The swimmer takes pride in doing the little things well and goes beyond the call of duty.
2. The swimmer demonstrates self-motivation.
3. The swimmer demonstrates an understanding and willingness to participate in drug-testing procedures.

Level 8

Championship Behavior and Accountability

1. The swimmer understands the relationship of seasonal, yearly, and quadrennial planning and works with the coach in establishing priorities.
2. The swimmer recognizes the importance of communicating with the media.
3. The swimmer accepts and appreciates the responsibility and benefits of being an ambassador of swimming by participating in public speaking, interviews, autograph sessions, etc.

Work Ethic and Self-Discipline

1. The swimmer demonstrates consistent, high-quality performance in training.
2. The swimmer can manage setbacks so they don't interfere with long-range goals.
3. The swimmer submits to drug testing without refusal.
4. The swimmer will consistently make choices that positively affect training performance.
5. The swimmer will actively participate in antidrug programs (e.g., leading by example, public speaking).

Psychological Skills

The factors that make up the psychological domain include arousal control, concentration, self-image, self-talk, imagery and visualization, goal setting, and meet and practice behaviors. These skills help the athlete develop the ability to focus on what he or she can control and not to worry about "uncontrollables."

Prerequisite

None

Level 1

Arousal Control

1. Understands and can demonstrate the difference between tense and relaxed muscles.
2. Can identify past situations where both have been present.

Concentration

1. Possesses a basic understanding of the concept of concentration.
2. Knows the difference between focusing on what's important and what's not.

Level 2

Arousal Control

1. Can describe the relationship between nervousness and performance.
2. Can describe the mind–body connection (negative thoughts → tight muscles → poor performance).

Self-Image

Understands the role of failure and the importance of learning from one's mistakes; understands that this is essential to becoming a champion.

Self-Talk

Has a general understanding of the effect that negative self-talk plays on performance (understands the concept of GIGO—garbage in, garbage out).

Mental Dimension of Training

Understands that an important part of training in swimming involves the mental dimension.

Concentration

1. Has an understanding of what to focus on and what to block out both in practice and in meets.
2. Is aware when focus leaves target and knows how to bring focus back (how to concentrate).

Level 3

Arousal Control

1. Understands the relationship between relaxation and performance.
2. Knows the three levels of nervousness (too little, just right, too much).
3. Can perform diaphragmatic (belly) breathing as relaxation technique.
4. Understands that stress comes from negative self-talk and faulty focus of concentration.
5. Understands the concept of "UCs," or uncontrollables, as a major source of stress.

Self-Talk

1. Understands the benefits of and uses positive self-talk and affirmations.
2. Closely monitors negative self-talk.

Concentration

Understands the importance of concentration in practice and meets and can regularly recognize a faulty focus and bring self back to a proper focus.

Goal Setting

Understands the value of setting goals to improve performance.

Self-Image

1. Is able to accept criticism from the coach.
2. Understands that criticism is a critique of skills, not a critique of an individual.

Level 4

Arousal Control

1. Can combine self-talk and slow breathing for arousal control.
2. Has a clear awareness of personal stressors (UCs).
3. Is capable of performing progressive muscle relaxation.
4. Recognizes that arousal can negatively affect mind and body.
5. Knows techniques to control mind (positive self-talk and imagery) and body (deep breathing, progressive muscle relaxation).

Imagery and Visualization

1. Understands the importance of imagery in enhancing performance.
2. Knows the principles behind effective imagery practice.
3. Can perform basic visualization skills.

Concentration

Can quickly return concentration focus in practice and in meets from uncontrollables to appropriate focus.

Goal Setting

1. Understands the principles of effective goal setting.
2. Beginning to set goals for the entire season.

Self-Talk

Knows at least one technique for handling negative self-talk.

Psychological Skills

Level 5

Arousal Control

1. Demonstrates an understanding of the individual zones of optimal functioning (IZOF) concept.
2. Can identify (personal) optimal zone of performance both in practice and competition.
3. Understands personal signs of under- or overarousal ("not enough" or "too much" nervousness).
4. Skilled in two or more arousal control techniques (see key terms in part I).

Imagery and Visualization

Can visualize a race from start to finish. Can control the image so vision matches actual performance.

Concentration

1. Develops a pre-race ritual or routine.
2. Develops race focal points for concentration.

Self-Image

1. Realizes that positive comments help reduce stress, build confidence, and can increase the enjoyment of competition and practice.
2. Understands the damage of negative self-talk to self-esteem, performance, and the enjoyment of the sport.

Goal Setting

1. Has developed a long-range goal within the sport.
2. Develops short-term and intermediate goals that ultimately tie into long-range goals.

Meet and Practice Behavior

1. Understands the effect of posture and actions on emotions.
2. Uses the "Act as if" strategy as a fallback position.

Level 6

Arousal Control

1. Demonstrates an understanding of factors that arouse and relax the athlete.
2. Utilizes relaxation techniques under meet duress to perform optimally.
3. Maintains optimum relaxation level ("good nervousness"), regardless of uncontrollables.
4. Learns to utilize imagery skills to manage competitive stress.

Imagery and Visualization

Through instruction is able to visualize a race from start to finish in complete detail (seeing, hearing, and feeling).

Self-Image and Goal Setting

Can use ultimate goal in sport to maintain intensity and work ethic in practice.

Concentration

1. Demonstrates an ability to rebound quickly from mistakes and failures.
2. Able to successfully use pre-race routines and control focal points to maintain concentration during a race.
3. Consistently swims "in own lane" in practice and meets.

Self-Talk

Able to positively reframe uncontrollables and adversity to enhance confidence.

Level 7

Arousal Control

1. Skilled at managing competitive pressure (uses relaxation techniques pre-race).
2. Maintains perspective before big meets and can have fun in big competitions.
3. Aware of tension in muscles and can relax them on cue as needed.
4. Develops and uses relaxation cues preperformance to maintain arousal control.

Imagery and Visualization

1. Can successfully utilize coping imagery for mastering stress.
2. Is able to create more vivid images in mind's eye.
3. Has developed control of internal images and can turn negatives into positives.
4. Can assess past races to develop peak performance cue.

Self-Image

1. Able to keep racing and swimming in perspective.
2. Does not tie up self-image in swim results.

Race Mentality

1. Understands that swimming fast is about not thinking.
2. Develops a sense of trust in self and abilities pre-race.
3. Learns to let the fast swim happen.

Goal Setting

1. Can utilize ultimate goal to persevere in the face of setbacks, obstacles, and losses.
2. Completely intrinsically driven.

Level 8

Arousal Control

1. Can raise or lower arousal control as needed before a competition.
2. Has developed own personal coping style integrating a number of relaxation techniques.
3. Can effectively handle national and international level pressure.
4. Has developed awareness of competitors' arousal level without being distracted.
5. Relaxation techniques perfected and utilized automatically as needed.

Imagery and Visualization

1. Able to utilize peak performance cues before races.
2. Displays ability to mentally rehearse in vivid detail and with imagery control.
3. Utilizes both mastery and coping imagery as needed.
4. Visualization skills perfected and used automatically as needed.

Self-Talk

1. Has the ability to swim fast despite the presence of last-second negative self-talk.
2. Can put self on "automatic" and quiet inner dialogue when racing.

Self-Image

1. Has developed inner sense of well-being from personal and athletic development.
2. Has a fully developed sense of mental toughness.

Concentration

1. Skill refined to "tunnel vision" as needed in practice and competition.
2. In total control of eyes and ears in terms of concentration.

two

Levels of Development

This chapter is in a chart form. Each chart illustrates one level all the way across each subject area. Although this is an easy way to look at an entire level seeing all categories at once, it is not meant to suggest that a swimmer must achieve all the criteria of one level before moving on to the next level.

It is important to keep in mind that all aspects of development do not occur at an exact rate and at the same time. We know that physical development occurs in spurts. An athlete may experience a big improvement in the training or the competitive components, but he or she may still lag behind in the psychological area.

Training

The workout sets listed in the training category are not intended to represent a full menu of sets for each of the energy systems. The critically important lactate tolerance sets and other anaerobic sets are not included because swimmers at any level can "keep up" with the long rest intervals. The intervals that are presented in the training category of this book represent the minimum pace that the swimmers must be able to sustain to handle the aerobic work in the next level. Needless to say, both the intervals and the length of the aerobic sets at any given level will vary throughout the season. As is the case with all of the other information presented in the book, coaches may need to modify these guidelines to suit the particular needs of their athletes and programs.

Competitive Performance

The competitive performance section is designed to allow the coach to establish a progression of times for the athlete to achieve in competition before the athlete can move to the next level. The focus is very light in the first three levels, which include the prerequisite level; performance times are introduced in level three. One of the goals in this category is to prepare the athlete for long-term development by emphasizing all four strokes, avoiding specialization until later in the athlete's career.

The competitive time progressions are designed to dovetail into what is expected in practice performances. The times listed next for each level are used to determine the training speeds in the training category.

Biomechanics

The biomechanical progressions emphasize technique acquisition in the development of swimmers. The goal here is not to dictate how technique should be taught but to provide a step-by-step developmental time line to keep athletes advancing throughout their careers.

The levels focus on both creation of propulsion through sculling and the minimization of water drag during training and races. Both factors are critical in improving overall swimming speed.

The distance per stroke cycle (one complete cycle, e.g., right-arm entry to right-arm entry in freestyle and backstroke) is very important to proper biomechanics and must be reinforced as the swimmer progresses through the developmental levels. Research continually shows that long distance per stroke is the most important factor in elite level swimming. Monitoring an athlete's distance per stroke cycle is the simplest, most objective tool that can be used in the field to assess biomechanical technique. Distance per stroke cycle should lengthen as technique improves.

Prerequisites

Training Set Requirements

Physical
Swims 25 yards in the prone or supine position from a push-off.

Competitive Performance

None

Biomechanical Progressions

1. Float face down for a period of one minute. (Swimmers may breathe when necessary, but they may not touch the bottom of the pool.)
2. Float face up with little or no movement for a period of one minute without touching the bottom of the pool.
3. From a standing position, or holding on to the side of the pool, demonstrate rhythmic breathing, exhaling underwater and inhaling above water.

Physiology

A variety of physiological adaptations are required for optimal performance because events in competitive swimming range in duration from about 20 seconds up to a little less than 20 minutes. Elements of both speed and endurance have been shown to be important factors in competitive success. Thus, competitive swimmers spend a great deal of their training efforts on enhancing their physiological capacities to optimize their sprint and endurance abilities. The development of physiological systems for success must coincide with the athlete's responsiveness to the various forms of conditioning at different times during his or her growth and development. For example, it has been shown that children have a limited capacity to perform and adapt to high-intensity anaerobic work prior to puberty. Thus, a well-planned training program designed to maximize the swimmers' ultimate performance potential will avoid placing too much emphasis on this kind of physiological conditioning until the late adolescent phase of development. Instead, the focus in early childhood should be in developing the skills and aerobic endurance necessary to perform the higher-intensity training later in the swimmers' careers. The physiological progressions included in this book were designed to reflect this philosophy by introducing physiological capacities at the appropriate times of the swimmer's career. In addition, field tests of physiological capacities are recommended instead of laboratory-based tests because of the lack of access to laboratory testing by most athletes and coaches. By taking this approach, we hope to provide guidance to our coaches and athletes and equip them with tools to evaluate the athletes' progress.

Character Development and Life Skills

Many coaches support learning life skills as a major benefit of participating in a swim program. These skills include such things as championship behavior and accountability, work ethic and self-discipline, time management, and commitment and loyalty. Ten years after a swimmer has stopped swimming the items most often mentioned about his or her swimming career are in this category. In our review of swimming literature, however, we did not find much information regarding at what level of a swimmer's career these issues should be addressed. As in all the other categories presented, each level builds upon the previous level.

Psychological Skills

The factors that make up the psychological domain include arousal control, concentration, self-image, self-talk, imagery and visualization, goal setting, and meet and practice behaviors. These skills help the athlete develop the ability to focus on what he or she can control and not to worry about "uncontrollables."

Physiological Progressions

None

Character Development and Life Skills

None

Psychological Skills

None

Level 1

Training Set Requirements

Physical

1. Swims 25 yards/meters of freestyle and backstroke.
2. Starts and finishes at the wall.

Cognitive

The swimmer begins to use the pace clock.

Competitive Performance

None

Biomechanical Progressions

Physical

1. From a push-off, maintain a prone streamlined body position, defined as positioning the body in a manner that reduces the resistance from the water. Streamlining should be applied during a start and push-off from the wall by using a tight "torpedo" position.
2. Hold this position for at least one and one-half body lengths and be able to vary the depth of the underwater push-off.
3. Execute a breakout from a push by holding the streamlined position; initiate a kicking action and progress to the surface of the water with a pull to the surface.
4. Propel forward in a prone position for at least one length of the pool.
5. Propel forward in a supine position for at least one length of the pool.
6. Maintain a vertical, stationary position with little or no leg movement in deep water, using a sculling motion.
7. Stroke progressions
   a. Complete progressions for the freestyle and backstroke.
   b. Begin to develop the butterfly and breaststroke.

Freestyle

   a. Complete the legal freestyle technique, using arms and legs for one length of the pool.
   b. Demonstrate shoulder and hip rolling motion during the freestyle stroke.
   c. Demonstrate the ability to comfortably take a breath on either the right or left side.

Backstroke

   a. Complete the legal backstroke technique, using arms and legs for one length of the pool.
   b. Demonstrate shoulder and hip rolling motion during the backstroke.

8. Demonstrate a proper dive from the side of the pool with a streamlined glide to the surface (follow the guidelines in the American Red Cross publication, *Safety Training for Swim Coaches*).
9. Perform an open turn either prone or supine where the hand touches the wall first, the body rotates to place the feet against the wall, the body drops underwater, and the swimmer pushes off in a streamlined position.

Cognitive

1. The swimmer knows which letter of the alphabet best describes the freestyle pulling pattern.
2. The swimmer can count up to five complete stroke cycles of freestyle.
3. The swimmer can count up to five complete stroke cycles of backstroke.

Physiological Progressions

Physical

1. Coordinated movement patterns: swims freestyle and backstroke with legal form.
2. Aerobic endurance
   a. Can complete a 30-minute practice session.
   b. Can perform a continuous swim for five minutes.

Character Development and Life Skills

Championship Behavior and Accountability

1. The swimmer understands he or she is part of a team and has respect for his or her teammates.
2. The swimmer listens to recommendations from the coach and tries to make the appropriate changes.
3. The swimmer understands appropriate team rules and the consequences of breaking the rules.

Work Ethic and Self-Discipline

1. The swimmer will pick up and put away any equipment he or she used in practice.
2. The swimmer will be ready to start practice on time with the appropriate equipment (suits, goggles, etc.).
3. The swimmer understands the importance of giving the coach his or her undivided attention while the coach is talking. The swimmer focuses his or her eyes on the coach and remains quiet when the coach is talking. The swimmer will also follow directions set forth by the coach in practice.
4. The swimmer will "Just say no!" to drugs and other harmful substances.
5. The swimmer will show respect for the facilities and equipment.

Time Management

The swimmer will arrive at practice sessions on time.

Commitment and Team Loyalty

1. The swimmer will know the team name and team colors.
2. The swimmer will know the names of teammates and coaches in his or her practice group.
3. The swimmer will know the name of any other training group(s) on the team besides his or her own group (e.g., age group 1, age group 2, senior, and national).

Psychological Skills

Arousal Control

1. Understands and can demonstrate the difference between tense and relaxed muscles.
2. Can identify past situations where both have been present.

Concentration

1. Possesses a basic understanding of what concentration is.
2. Knows the difference between focusing on what's important and what's not.

Level 2

Training Set Requirements

Physical

Can complete the following practice sets:

6 × 50 Free

6 × 50 Back

6 × 50 Breast

6 × 50 Fly

6 × 50 Kick

Cognitive

The swimmer accurately counts and computes distances.

Competitive Performance

Has participated in competitive situations for the primary purpose of skill development (i.e., time trials, intrasquad meets, dual meets, and other entry level competitions).

Biomechanical Progressions

Physical

1. Execute a start from the blocks. Hold the underwater streamlined position for one and one-half body lengths; initiate a kicking action for one body length and progress to the surface of the water with a pull.
2. Execute a legal freestyle, backstroke, butterfly, and breaststroke turn including an approach of at least 10 yards/meters.
3. Stroke progression: Complete progressions for butterfly and breaststroke.

Butterfly

a. Complete one length of the pool with legal butterfly form.

b. Demonstrate correct timing of the pull, kick, and breath during the butterfly.

c. Demonstrate an undulating motion during the butterfly stroke.

Breaststroke

a. Complete one length of the pool with legal breaststroke form.

b. Demonstrate correct timing of the pull, kick, and breath during the breaststroke.

4. Perform 100 yards/meters individual medley with legal technique.

Cognitive

1. From a push the swimmer counts the number of stroke cycles of freestyle, and the coach records the time for one length of the pool.
2. From a push the swimmer counts the number of stroke cycles of backstroke, and the coach records the time for one length of the pool.
3. From a push the swimmer counts the number of stroke cycles of butterfly, and the coach records the time for one length of the pool.
4. From a push the swimmer counts the number of stroke cycles of breaststroke, and the coach records the time for one length of the pool.

Physiological Progressions

Physical

1. Coordinated movement patterns: swims all four strokes.
2. Aerobic endurance: can perform continuous swim for 10 minutes.

Cognitive

The swimmer begins to understand maturation, physical development, and nutrition.

a. Understands and accepts individual differences in physical size within an age group.
b. Understands that energy for exercise is derived from nutrition.

Character Development and Life Skills

Championship Behavior and Accountability

1. The swimmer demonstrates an understanding of sportsmanship–championship behavior (e.g., doesn't throw goggles, congratulates opponents).
2. The swimmer will treat teammates, parents, and coaches like the swimmer would want to be treated.
3. The swimmer talks to the coach before and after each race.

Work Ethic and Self-Discipline

During practice the swimmer will

a. leave on time during sets,
b. start and finish at the wall,
c. swim the set in the prescribed manner (e.g., doesn't do freestyle on butterfly sets, doesn't pull on kicking sets, performs all turns legally),
d. swim the entire set (doesn't walk on the bottom of the pool, counts accurately), and
e. communicate with his or her coach.

Time Management

1. The swimmer understands the importance of doing quality work in the classroom and will complete his or her homework on time.
2. The swimmer will turn in appropriate team paperwork in a timely fashion (meet entries, release forms, change of address, etc.).

Commitment and Team Loyalty

1. The swimmer will learn the history of the team.
2. The swimmer chooses a swimming hero (may be a member of his or her team) and knows the event in which the hero competed or competes.
3. The swimmer takes pride in being a member of his or her team, which the swimmer demonstrates by
   a. participating in team cheers,
   b. knowing the coaches' names, and
   c. supporting and cheering on teammates during swims (practice or meets).

Psychological Skills

Arousal Control

1. Can describe the relationship between nervousness and performance.
2. Can describe the mind–body connection (negative thoughts → tight muscles → poor performance).

Self-Image

Understands the role of failure and learning from mistakes; perceives that this is essential to becoming a champion.

Self-Talk

Has a general understanding of the effect that negative self-talk plays on performance (understands the concept of "GIGO"—garbage in, garbage out).

Mental Dimension of Training

Understands that an important part of training in swimming involves the mental dimension.

Concentration

1. Has an understanding of what to focus on and what to block out both in practice and in meets.
2. Has an awareness of when focus leaves target and can bring focus back (knows how to concentrate).

Level 3

Training Set Requirements

Physical

Can complete the following practice sets:

Ages 10 and under

	LCM	SCY
3 × 200 IM on	4:20	3:50
6 × 100 Kick on	2:20	2:10
8 × 100 Free on	2:00	1:50
And any one of the following sets:		
12 × 100 Free on	1:55	1:45
6 × 100 Fly on	2:20	2:10
12 × 100 Back on	2:10	2:00
12 × 100 Breast on	2:20	2:10

Ages 11-12

	LCM	SCY
4 × 200 IM on	4:10	3:45
7 × 100 Kick on	2:20	2:10
10 × 100 Free on	1:50	1:40
And any one of the following sets:		
16 × 100 Free on	1:45	1:35
9 × 100 Fly on	2:10	2:00
16 × 100 Back on	2:00	1:50
16 × 100 Breast on	2:10	2:00

Ages 13 and over

	LCM	SCY
6 × 200 IM on	4:00	3:40
8 × 100 Kick on	2:20	2:10
12 × 100 Free on	1:45	1:35
And any one of the following sets:		
16 × 100 Free on	1:35	1:25
12 × 100 Fly on	2:00	1:50
16 × 100 Back on	1:50	1:40
16 × 100 Breast on	2:00	1:50

Competitive Performance

Has competed in all the events offered in his or her age group and has met all of the following time standards (in yards or meters) in a sanctioned USA Swimming Meet.

	LCM	SCY
100 Free	1:20	1:10
100 Back	1:35	1:25
100 Breast	1:50	1:35
100 Fly	1:40	1:25
200 IM	3:20	2:55

Biomechanical Progressions

Physical

Perform a legal 200 individual medley swim.

Cognitive

1. Complete one length of freestyle holding the same time or faster but using at least one less stroke cycle than in level 2.
2. Complete one length of backstroke holding the same time or faster but using at least one less stroke cycle than in level 2.
3. Complete one length of butterfly holding the same time or faster but using at least one less stroke cycle than in level 2.
4. Complete one length of breaststroke holding the same time or faster but using at least one less stroke cycle than in level 2.

Physiological Progressions

Physical

Coordinated movement patterns: swims all four strokes with legal form.

Aerobic endurance

Performs T30 or other threshold set one time per season.

Cognitive

1. Understands maturation and physical development: begins to understand the relationship between training programs and maturation and physical development.
2. Understands the purpose of heart rate measurement.
3. Can measure his or her own resting and exercise heart rate.
4. Understands the importance of muscular flexibility in swimming performance.

Character Development and Life Skills

Championship Behavior and Accountability

The swimmer will demonstrate a higher level of sportsmanship—championship behavior than in level 2 (e.g., respects competitors and gets along with friends regardless of ability level).

Work Ethic and Self-Discipline

1. The swimmer attends the recommended meets and understands the importance of being on time for meet warm-ups.
2. The swimmer meets the established attendance requirements.
3. The swimmer understands why he or she must "Just say no!" to drugs and other harmful substances.
4. The swimmer learns to challenge him- or herself to perform to the utmost of his or her ability in practice.

Time Management

Demonstrates an ability to balance school and outside activities.

Commitment and Loyalty

The swimmer chooses a national swimming hero and knows the event in which the hero competed or competes.

Psychological Skills

Arousal Control

1. Understands the relationship between relaxation and performance.
2. Knows the three levels of nervousness (too little, just right, too much).
3. Can perform diaphragmatic (belly) breathing as a relaxation technique.
4. Understands that stress comes from self-talk and faulty focus of concentration.
5. Understands the concept of "UCs," or "uncontrollables," as a major source of stress.

Self-Talk

1. Understands the benefits of and uses positive self-talk and affirmations.
2. Closely monitors negative self-talk.

Concentration

Understands the importance of concentration in practice and meets and can regularly recognize a faulty focus and bring self back to a proper focus.

Goal Setting

Understands the value of setting goals to improve performance.

Self-Image

1. Is able to accept criticism from coach.
2. Understands that criticism is a critique of an individual's skills, not a critique of the person.

Level 4

Training Set Requirements

Physical

Can complete the following practice sets:

	LCM	SCY
6 × 200 IM on	3:40	3:20
8 × 100 Kick on	2:10	2:00
16 × 100 Freestyle on	1:40	1:30

And any one of the following sets:

	LCM	SCY
20 × 100 Free on	1:30	1:20
20 × 100 Back on	1:40	1:30
20 × 100 Breast on	1:50	1:40
20 × 100 Fly on	1:40	1:30

Competitive Performance

Has competed in all the events offered in his or her age group and has met all of the following time standards (in yards or meters) in a sanctioned USA Swimming Meet.

	LCM	SCY
100 Free	1:15	1:05
200 Free	2:40	2:20
400/500 Free	5:20	6:00
800/1000 Free	10:40	12:00
1500/1650 Free	20:00	19:45
100 Back	1:25	1:15
100 Breast	1:35	1:25
100 Fly	1:25	1:15
200 IM	3:00	2:40

Biomechanical Progressions

Physical

1. Complete one length of each stroke holding the same time or faster and using fewer stroke cycles than in level 3.
2. Maintain consistent stroke rates and times in training sets.

Cognitive

1. The swimmer understands the relationship between distance per stroke, stroke rate, and swimming speed.
2. The swimmer can name two ways to minimize resistance or drag from the water.
3. The swimmer can explain one reason why sculling is important in creating propulsion.

Physiological Progressions

Physical

Aerobic endurance: swims a T30 or other threshold set two times per season with improvement.

Cognitive

1. Understands the concept of a balanced diet and the basic fuels used during swimming training.
2. Begins to understand the basics of different energy system usage in sprinting versus distance swimming.
3. Can measure heart rate to monitor exercise intensity and recovery.

Character Development and Life Skills

Championship Behavior and Accountability

The swimmer will know the names of his or her competitors.

Work Ethic and Self-Discipline

1. The swimmer is not influenced by the negative behavior of his or her teammates.
2. The swimmer takes responsibility for attendance, performance, and practice habits and understands how these three relate to meet performance.

Psychological Skills

Arousal Control

1. Can combine self-talk and slow breathing for arousal control.
2. Has a clear awareness of personal stressors (UCs).
3. Is capable of performing progressive muscle relaxation.
4. Recognizes that arousal can negatively affect mind and body.
5. Knows techniques to control the mind (positive self-talk and imagery) and the body (deep breathing, progressive muscle relaxation).

Imagery and Visualization

1. Understands the importance of imagery in enhancing performance.
2. Knows the principles behind effective imagery practice.
3. Can perform basic visualization skills.

Concentration

Can quickly return concentration focus in practice and in meets from "uncontrollables" to the appropriate focus.

Goal Setting

1. Understands the principles of effective goal setting.
2. Beginning to set goals for the entire season.

Self-Talk

Knows at least one technique for handling negative self-talk.

Level 5

Training Set Requirements

Physical

Can complete the following practice sets:

	LCM	SCY
4 × 400 IM on	6:40	6:00
12 × 100 Kick on	2:00	1:50
24 × 100 Free on	1:30	1:20

And any one of the following sets:

	LCM	SCY
24 × 100 Free on	1:20	1:10
24 × 100 Back on	1:30	1:20
24 × 100 Breast on	1:40	1:30
24 × 100 Fly on	1:30	1:20

Competitive Performance

Must achieve at least one time standard from the Age Group Time Standards, Championship Based Standards, level 1. (See the current *USA Swimming Rules & Regulations* for time standards, or check the USA Swimming web page at http://www.usa-swimming.org./)

Biomechanical Progressions

Physical

Perform a 400 individual medley swim with correct transitions between strokes.

Cognitive

The swimmer, with the assistance of his or her coach, can calculate swimming speed and distance per stroke during competition and training.

Physiological Progressions

Physical

1. Muscular strength and endurance: can perform sit-ups, push-ups, and pull-ups (chin-ups).
2. Aerobic endurance: swims a T30 or other threshold set three times per season with continuous improvement.
3. Sprint capacity/CP system: swims 12 × 25 (three butterfly, three backstroke, three breaststroke, and three freestyle) on 3:00 (3 per stroke) at maximum velocity three times per season.

Cognitive

1. Knowledge of energy systems: can explain aerobic and anaerobic systems of energy delivery.
2. Understands nutritional requirements of training and competition: demonstrates understanding of basic nutrition principles, fuels for swimming performance, training diets, hydration, RDAs for swimmers, and the importance of eating a balanced diet.
3. Demonstrates an understanding of the relationship between training programs and maturation and development and their effects on competitive and training performance.
4. Understands how to use heart rate measurement to monitor training progress.

Character Development and Life Skills

Championship Behavior and Accountability

The swimmer learns to accept responsibility for his or her performance.

Work Ethic and Self-Discipline

1. The swimmer will learn coping strategies to deal with peer pressure.
2. The swimmer will learn coping strategies to deal with parent pressure.
3. The swimmer will be able to list the five classes of prohibited substances.
4. The swimmer understands and performs personal race strategies.

Time Management

The swimmer demonstrates an ability to balance school, social activities, swimming, and family.

Commitment and Team Loyalty

1. The swimmer can effectively communicate his or her commitment to his or her parents, coach, and teammates.
2. The swimmer knows the team goals and will take an active part in developing specific and attainable practice group goals.
3. The swimmer understands the relationship between his or her personal commitment level and results.

Psychological Skills

Arousal Control

1. Demonstrates an understanding of the individual zones of optimal functioning (IZOF) concept.
2. Can identify (personal) optimal zone of performance both in practice and in competition.
3. Understands personal signs of under- or over-arousal ("not enough" or "too much" nervousness).
4. Skilled in two or more arousal control techniques (see the key terms at the end of part I).

Imagery and Visualization

Can visualize a race from start to finish. Can control the image so the vision matches actual performance.

Concentration

1. Develops a pre-race ritual or routine.
2. Develops race focal points for concentration.

Self-Image

1. Realizes that positive comments help reduce stress, build confidence, and can increase enjoyment of competition and practice.
2. Understands the damage of negative self-talk to self-esteem, performance, and the enjoyment of the sport.

Goal Setting

1. Has developed a long-range goal within the sport.
2. Develops short-term and intermediate goals that ultimately tie into long-range goals.

Meet and Practice Behavior

1. Understands the effect of posture and actions on emotions.
2. Uses the "Act as if" strategy as a fallback position.

Level 6

Training Set Requirements

Physical

Can complete the following practice sets:

	LCM
4 × 400 IM on	6:20
12 × 100 Kick on	1:55
24 × 100 Free on	1:25

And any one of the following:

24 × 100 Free on	1:15
24 × 100 Back on	1:25
24 × 100 Breast on	1:35
24 × 100 Fly on	1:25

Competitive Performance

Meets a Junior Championship Time Standard in one or more individual events. (See the current *USA Swimming Rules & Regulations* for time standards, or check the USA Swimming web page at http://www.usa-swimming.org/.)

Biomechanical Progressions

Physical

1. Continues to decrease the number of stroke cycles or swim faster with the same number of cycles.
2. Decreases the number of cycles per length during competition.

Cognitive

The swimmer can calculate swimming speed, distance per stroke, and stroke rate.

Physiological Progressions

Physical

1. Muscular strength and endurance: can perform sit-ups, push-ups, and pull-ups (chin-ups) with improvement from previous level.
2. Aerobic endurance: performs T30 or other threshold set three times per season with continuous improvement.
3. Lactate tolerance: performs a set of 12 × 100 (or until failure) on 2:30 holding current best 200 pace (2nd 100 split) three times per season with continuous improvement.
4. Sprint capacity/CP system: performs 12 × 25 on 3:00 (specialty stroke) at maximum velocity.

Cognitive

1. The swimmer demonstrates knowledge of energy systems.
    a. Can describe the relationship between training sets and energy systems.
    b. Demonstrates understanding of training periodization.
2. The swimmer understands the nutritional requirements of training and competition.

Character Development and Life Skills

Championship Behavior and Accountability

The swimmer accepts the responsibility of being a leader and/or role model. The swimmer leads by being a positive example.

Work Ethic and Self-Discipline

1. The swimmer is able to explain the rationale of the five categories of banned substances.
2. The swimmer demonstrates an understanding of the short- and long-term effects of performance-enhancing drugs.

Time Management

The swimmer has mastered time management skills so outside activities do not interfere with practice and meet attendance.

Commitment and Team Loyalty

1. The swimmer understands the need to sacrifice self-interest for team goals.
2. The swimmer demonstrates commitment to his or her team by continued dedicated membership.

Psychological Skills

Arousal Control

1. Demonstrates an understanding of factors that arouse and relax the athlete.
2. Utilizes relaxation techniques under meet duress to perform optimally.
3. Maintains optimum relaxation level ("good" nervousness), regardless of uncontrollables.
4. Learns to utilize imagery skills to manage competitive stress.

Imagery and Visualization

Through instruction the swimmer is able to visualize a race from start to finish in complete detail (seeing, hearing, and feeling).

Self-Image and Goal Setting

Can utilize ultimate goal in sport to maintain intensity and work ethic in practice.

Concentration

1. Demonstrates an ability to quickly rebound from mistakes and failures.
2. Able to successfully use pre-race routines and control focal points during a race to maintain concentration.
3. Consistently swims "in own lane" in practice and meets.

Self-Talk

Able to positively reframe uncontrollables and adversity to enhance confidence.

Level 7

Training Set Requirements

Physical

Can complete the following practice sets:

	LCM
4 × 400 IM on	6:00
12 × 100 Kick on	1:50
24 × 100 Free on	1:20

And any one of the following:

24 × 100 Free on	1:12 (Women) 1:08 (Men)
24 × 100 Back on	1:20 (Women) 1:15 (Men)
24 × 100 Breast on	1:30 (Women) 1:25 (Men)
24 × 100 Fly on	1:20 (Women) 1:15 (Men)

Competitive Performance

Meets a National Championship Time Standard in one or more individual events. (See current *USA Swimming Rules & Regulations* for time standards, or check the USA Swimming web page at http://www.usa-swimming.org/.)

Biomechanical Progressions

Physical

Continues to improve distance per stroke and/or swimming speed during competition and training.

Physiological Progressions

Physical

1. Muscular strength and endurance: demonstrates improvement in muscular endurance (stroke specific).
2. Aerobic endurance: performs a T30 or other threshold set three times per season with continuous improvement.
3. Lactate tolerance: performs a set of 12 × 100 (or until failure) on 2:30 holding current best 200 pace (2nd 100 split) three times per season with continuous improvement.
4. Sprint capacity/CP system: performs 12 × 25 on 3:00 (specialty stroke) at maximum velocity three times per season with continuous improvement.

Cognitive

1. The swimmer demonstrates knowledge of energy systems.
    a. Demonstrates knowledge of personal training velocities for each training category.
    b. Can discuss training needs based on test-set results.
2. The swimmer develops and understands a nutritional plan for training and competition.

Character Development and Life Skills

Championship Behavior and Accountability

1. The swimmer demonstrates leadership responsibilities by working with younger swimmers (e.g., giving talks, water work).
2. The swimmer understands the importance of seasonal, yearly, and quadrennial planning and the consistency of the plan within each of the cycles.
3. The swimmer recognizes the effects of poor communication.

Work Ethic and Self-Discipline

1. The swimmer takes pride in doing the little things well and goes beyond the call of duty.
2. The swimmer demonstrates self-motivation.
3. The swimmer demonstrates an understanding of and is willing to participate in drug testing procedures.

Psychological Skills

Arousal Control

1. Skilled at managing competitive pressure (uses relaxation techniques pre-race).
2. Maintains perspective before big meets and can have fun in big competitions.
3. Is aware of tension in muscles and can relax them on cue as needed.
4. Develops and uses relaxation cues preperformance to maintain arousal control.

Imagery and Visualization

1. Can successfully utilize coping imagery for mastering stress.
2. Is able to create more vivid images in his or her mind.
3. Has developed control of internal images and can turn negatives into positives.
4. Can assess past races to develop peak performance cues.

Self-Image

1. Able to keep racing and swimming in perspective.
2. Does not tie up self-image in swim results.

Race Mentality

1. Understands that swimming fast is about not thinking.
2. Develops a sense of trust in self and abilities pre-race.
3. Learns to let the fast swim happen.

Goal Setting

1. Can utilize ultimate goal to persevere in the face of setbacks, obstacles, and losses.
2. Completely intrinsically driven.

Level 8

Training Set Requirements

Physical

Can complete the following practice sets:

	LCM
4 × 400 IM on	5:40
12 × 100 Kick on	1:45
24 × 100 Free on	1:15

Competitive Performance

Ranked among the Top 8 fastest swimmers in the world or is a member of the USA Olympic Team.

Biomechanical Progressions

Physical

Continues to improve distance per stroke and/or swimming speed during competition and training.

Physiological Progressions

Physical

1. Muscular strength and endurance
   a. Demonstrates maintenance of muscular strength.
   b. Demonstrates improvement in stroke-specific muscular endurance.
2. Aerobic endurance: performs a T30 or other threshold set three times per season with continuous improvement.
3. Lactate tolerance: demonstrates ability to perform a set of 12 × 100 (or until failure) on 2:30 holding current best 200 pace (2nd 100 split) three times per season with continuous improvement.
4. Sprint capacity/CP system: performs 12 × 25 on 3:00 (specialty stroke) at maximum velocity three times per season with continuous improvement.

Cognitive

The swimmer understands the nutritional requirements of training and competition: demonstrates ability to apply nutritional information to daily living.

Character Development and Life Skills

Championship Behavior and Accountability

1. The swimmer understands the relationship of seasonal, yearly, and quadrennial planning and works with the coach in establishing priorities.
2. The swimmer recognizes the importance of communicating with the media.
3. The swimmer accepts and appreciates the responsibility and benefits of being an ambassador of swimming by participating in public speaking, interviews, autographs, etc.

Work Ethic and Self-Discipline

1. The swimmer demonstrates consistent, high-quality performance in training.
2. The swimmer can manage setbacks so they don't interfere with long-range goals.
3. The swimmer submits to drug testing without refusal.
4. The swimmer consistently makes choices that positively affect training performances.
5. The swimmer participates actively in antidrug programs (e.g., leading by example, public speaking).

Psychological Skills

Arousal Control

1. Can raise or lower arousal control as needed before a competition.
2. Has developed own personal coping style integrating a number of relaxation techniques.
3. Can effectively handle national and international level pressure.
4. Has developed awareness of competitors' arousal level without being distracted.
5. Has perfected relaxation techniques and utilizes them automatically as needed.

Imagery and Visualization

1. Able to utilize peak performance cue before races.
2. Displays ability to mentally rehearse in vivid detail and with imagery control.
3. Utilizes both mastery and coping imagery as needed.
4. Visualization skills perfected and used automatically as needed.

Self-Talk

1. Has the ability to swim fast despite the presence of last-second negative self-talk.
2. Can put self on "automatic" and quiet inner dialogue when racing.

Self-Image

1. Has developed inner sense of well-being from personal athletic development.
2. Has fully developed a sense of mental toughness.

Concentration

1. Skill refined to "tunnel vision" as needed in practice and competition.
2. In total control of eyes and ears in terms of concentration.

PART II

Progressions for Coach Development

Part II provides general concepts for the coach about how to develop five of the areas covered in part I. The competitive performance category is not included in part II because it is an outcome of the other five areas. Progressions for Coach Development is the "Cliff notes" to coaching. It expands on the five developmental areas and provides the coach basic information to help his or her athletes progress through the levels.

Each chapter in part II covers a specific developmental area. It was deemed almost impossible to separate the in-depth material to mimic the level layout of chapter 2 because so much of the material builds upon itself. Each of the chapters in part II provide both theoretical and practical information to augment the skills listed in part I.

Some of the material presented in the following chapters is very technical in nature and not necessarily meant to be used or understood by a first-time or entry-level coach. As a coach progresses in his or her career this material may become more relevant.

three

Training

Tom Avischious, Larry Herr, and Jaci VanHeest, PhD

When athletes compete, the outcome of the performance is the first thing that draws everyone's attention. The last-second field goal in football, the half-court basketball shot with the clock reading ":00," or the last 50 meters of the 200-meter freestyle can all be very memorable. These competitive experiences are all the result or product of something much more. That something is the training or the process that goes into those performances. "Getting there is the work; performing is the reward" is a very common saying in competitive athletics. This chapter focuses on the "getting there" part (or training) and the general concepts that a coach may use in planning for a competitive swimming season.

Developing a Young Swimmer Throughout His or Her Career

Participation in sport was designed to develop a sense of enjoyment, inclusion, and mastery. Age, gender, maturation, or ability was not intended to limit a child's ability to acquire and develop the technical elements necessary for success. The focus of any age group program should not merely be to allow children to experience a sport but also to develop their technical expertise systematically. Therefore, a coach must take the long-term developmental approach when designing a child's training program.

Listed next are some general guidelines for sport participation. They are designed to be progressive from infancy to adulthood based on growth and development literature. General categories included are motor skills, learning skills, and sport participation and activities. Table 3.1 is designed to provide more specific information regarding the development of the technical aspects of swimming. Included with the overall guideline is a glossary of terms that have been used in the categorization of development.

Key Terms

Motor skills

- Complex—Combinations of fundamental and transitional skills (e.g., a basketball layup, including the run, jump, and throw for accuracy).
- Fundamental—Basic skills essential for future motor activity (e.g., kicking and pulling in swimming).
- Postural—Automatic response to a change in position (balance maintenance).
- Transitional—Combination of fundamental skills (swimming for distance).
- Voluntary—Conscious movement (hand–eye coordination).

Learning Skills

- Closed system—Constant conditions; very few adjustments necessary.
- Open system—Dynamic conditions; constantly responding to varying stimuli or choices.

Sport Participation and Activities

- Game—Play requiring skill.
- Sport—Games requiring physical exertion usually with some rules.
- Competitive sports—Youth sports organized to establish winners and losers (generally involves levels, divisions, competitions, play-offs, etc.).
- Youth sports—Structured, organized programs designed by adults for children (can be either individual or team sport).

Seasonal Training

An important consideration for a coach to make when designing a training plan is to determine how many seasons the swimmer will have in a year. USA Swimming recognizes two competitive seasons within one year. Many swimmers are also members of other organizations that have their own competitive seasons; examples include summer league, high school, and NCAA swimming. To properly achieve maximum development in a career, a swimmer should definitely consider a year-round commitment to the sport (level 3 in the Progressions for Athlete Development).

One of the two competitive seasons for USA Swimming members is a winter or short-course season that is generally swum in a 25-yard pool. The short-course season usually runs from September through April and is clearly the longer of the two seasons. In most successful USA Swim-

Table 3.1

Sport participation category (development stage)	Training objective(s)	Metabolic or physiological focus	Biomechanical or technical focus	Psychological or social focus	Training load imposed
Reflexive awareness (0-2 years)	Stimulation of body	Kinesthetic awareness		Enjoy feeling their body movements	
Motor memory development (3-6 years)	Motor pattern development (e.g., "Feel for the water")	Kinesthetic awareness	Using appropriate stroke patterns	Having fun	
Sport preparation (6-9 years)	Stroke technique, aerobic development	Aerobic conditioning	Efficient technique	Joy of participation, developmental progression	2-3 x per week, 1500-4000 m/wk
Sport delineation (9-12 years)	Technique development, aerobic base, muscular endurance	Aerobic 95%, threshold 50%, anaerobic up to 5%	Efficient technique	Competition behavior, teamwork, maturational differences	3-6 x per week, 5000-40000 m/wk
(12-14 years)	Aerobic maintenance, technique	Aerobic 95%, threshold > 50%, anaerobic up to 5%; increase pace of threshold	Efficient technique, integration of physiology and mechanics	Teamwork, motivation (intrinsic) and social group	6-10 x per week, 30,000-60,000 m/wk
Sport mastery (14-20 years)	Integration of efficient biomechanics and physiology	Aerobic 95%, threshold > 50%, anaerobic up to 5%; increase pace of threshold	Efficient technique	Teamwork, motivation, knowledge of body and training	8-12 x per week, 40,000-100,000 m/wk
Elite mastery (17-24+ years)	Integration of efficient biomechanics and physiology	Aerobic 95%, threshold > 50%, anaerobic to 5%: increase pace of threshold	Efficient technique	Teamwork, motivation, overtraining and and psychology, competition stress	Event-length specific

ming programs, the bulk of the training will be done during the short-course season.

The second season or long-course season is generally swum in a long-course pool or 50-meter pool. The summer season usually runs from April to the middle of August. Although the summer is the shorter of the two seasons, its significance should not be overlooked. During this season, most competitions are held in 50-meter pools. This is important because most international meets and all Olympic games are swum in this course. How well swimmers perform in this course may be a good indication of future potential success at the highest level of national and international meets.

Despite the differences of competition courses and the lengths of each season, the two seasons should be considered together as one part of a long-term program of development. There may be some swimmers who are slightly better at the short-course or the long-course season. The two seasons break up the year into more manageable parts for both the coach and the swimmer. Most important, the overall plan should be constructed to combine the two seasons to progress the athlete throughout the year.

It is important to chart a course of action for the season based on the goals and objectives for each of your athletes. Many methods can be used to develop a seasonal plan; however, the following series of questions should be considered:

1. Which changes need to be induced in the swimmer?
2. Which types of workout sets and/or exercises will induce these changes?
3. Which training methods need to be used?
4. How do you ensure an appropriate training load?
5. How are the influences of subsequent training sessions combined?
6. How do you relate training sessions and time for recovery?

The method typically used to develop the seasonal plan is described in cycles. Periodization of training is a common method used by coaches in many cyclical sports such as cycling, running, weight training, and swimming. The training cycles can be divided into the following three primary categories:

1. **Macrocycle**—The largest period of time that will allow your athlete to peak for performance. Typically this is one season or one year in duration.
2. **Mesocycle**—The mesocycle is a period of months or weeks within the macrocycle. This is a period where specific training goals are established and achieved.
3. **Microcycle**—The microcycle is a period of weeks or days within the mesocycle. The specific daily workouts are developed within the microcycle to focus on specific adaptation.

Each of the specific cycles is illustrated in figure 3.1.

Overload and adaptation in an athlete can be caused in many ways. It is important for a coach to understand the concepts of individual differences and overload. Application of these principles will enable a coach to apply appropriate training loads to swimmers.

Individual Differences

Each swimmer will adapt to the training load in her or his own way and time line. This is one

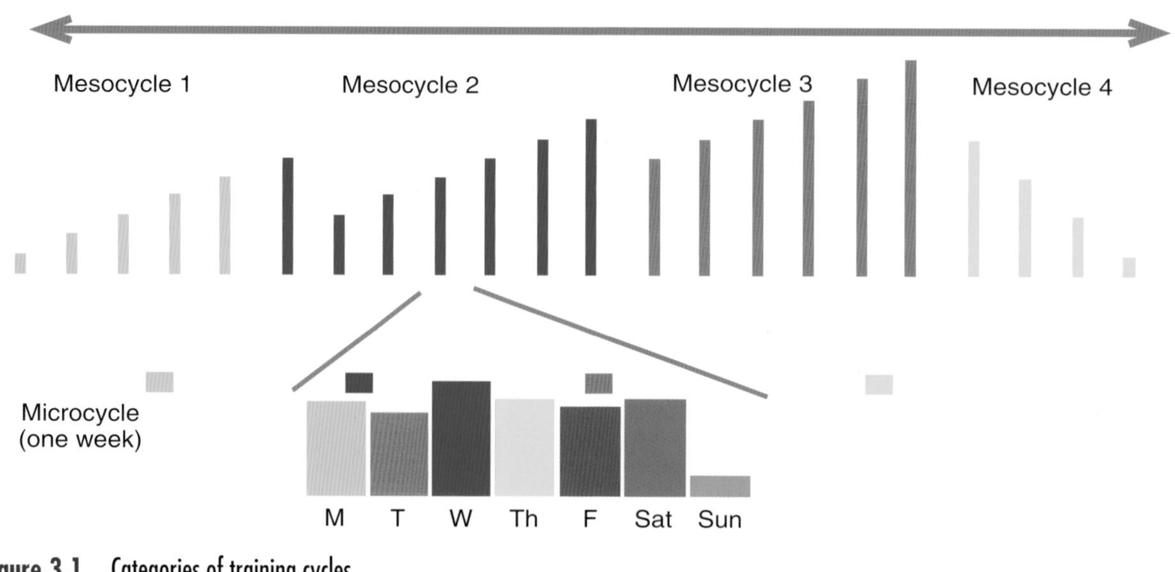

Figure 3.1 Categories of training cycles.

reason for testing your swimmers' adaptation regularly with test protocols or test sets. Other areas of individual differences include consideration of the following: fitness level, age, gender, stroke specialty, distance orientation, and the goals of each swimmer.

A coach should try to assess the fitness level of a swimmer before he or she develops a training plan. Look at the swimmer's cardiovascular system and determine the efficiency of the heart and lungs to handle physical exercise. The fitness level, through training, should adapt to the extra stress and should improve. This marker is a general term applied to sports, but its significance can largely influence the potential success of an athlete. Fitness levels can especially be influenced by the age of the athlete.

The age of the swimmer has a big impact on training. Chronological age and biological age are the two types of ages that a coach needs to consider. The chronological age of an individual is the physical age or years since birth. Biological age refers to the anatomical growth and development of the individual. Of the two, biological age probably has the bigger influence on training because everyone matures at different times. A coach should try to match the training development phases with a swimmer's biological development. This timing is important to maximize the potential of each swimmer in a training program.

The relationship between biological age and gender is also important for coaches to consider because boys and girls mature at different rates. The maturation process can greatly affect training as well as performance. As an individual matures he or she not only grows taller but also stronger. These two factors influence a swimmer's physiological response to training as well as his or her stroke technique.

As a swimmer becomes older, a coach also needs to be aware of differences in stroke specialty. The two main components of specialty to consider are related to distance (sprint, middle, distance) and stroke (fly, back, breast, free). The integration of these two factors should not only be made in the yearly plan but also in the daily plan. The length of time to reach peak performance is generally shorter in distance events. Therefore, the timing of training development may need to be adjusted as coaches deem it necessary. The primary stroke of the swimmer has less of an influence in the training plan. It is important for coaches to design sets that stress stroke work so a swimmer will be prepared to handle the demands of competition. For younger swimmers, a good training tool is the frequent use of individual medley (IM) training sets to foster development in all four competitive strokes.

A coach and swimmer need to work together to determine the swimmer's goals for reaching his or her peak performance. Training should then be designed to allow the swimmer an opportunity to achieve his or her goal(s) at the end of each season, year, or career.

Many more factors could be discussed here, but this section addresses some of the more important ones. As a coach gains more experience, he or she can better see how to handle the obstacles that arise when designing a plan. The coach always needs to consider how to get the most out of each swimmer. It is through training that those desired successes become reality.

Workout Design

Overload is a larger than normal training workload. This load is a progressive stress on the individual beyond what is a natural stimulus resulting in adaptation. The workload must be large enough to stress the individual or break down the swimmer but not to the extent that the athlete cannot adapt.

Application of the principles of overload and individual differences can be applied using various strategies to train swimmers. Two common types of training (continuous training and interval training) are described next.

Continuous Training

Continuous training is straight swimming without a rest interval. There are two general types of continuous training—slow-paced and fast-paced. In most swimming programs, continuous training is used for warm-up or cool-down periods. The T30, or 3,000 for time, swim would be considered continuous training as well as a test set. Fast-paced continuous training (typically 80 to 90 percent of the maximum heart rate) is difficult and should be considered carefully when designing training programs.

Interval Training

Interval training consists of periods of work followed by rest intervals. Four primary components

listed next are involved in interval training design. Depending on the manner in which these four components are manipulated, aerobic or anaerobic pathways will be primarily taxed by the set.

1. Training or swim distance
2. Training interval or work time
3. Recovery interval (rest or recovery period between swims)
4. Repetitions of the exercise (number of swims)

It is important to design the daily training program to achieve a specific training goal that is incorporated into the overall training plan.

Using Language That All Coaches Will Understand

Swimming is dependent upon the constant generation of energy by the skeletal muscle. Without energy, the athlete will be unable to move in the water. The pathways are designed along a line. The processes always begin at the top of the line and flow down the pathways.

Energy can be generated within the body in several ways, but three primary pathways are important to understand. These three are the ATP-CP, anaerobic glycolysis, and aerobic pathways.

ATP-CP Pathway

Production of energy is the goal of metabolism. Energy is needed to enable muscles to contract. The demand for energy is related to the intensity of the work placed on the body. If the energy demand is high, the body must generate energy very rapidly. To accomplish this task, muscle cells contain immediately accessible fuel stores—ATP (adenosine triphosphate) and CP (creatine phosphate). ATP and CP are energy-rich fuel stores that are contained within the muscle cells. These fuels are limited in supply. High-intensity work, therefore, can be maintained for relatively short periods of time (less than 10 seconds) and at the start of exercise. After ATP and CP are reduced to a low level another energy-producing pathway must contribute for muscular contraction to continue.

The ATP-CP system provides some energy for all swim distances. The portion of the total energy output by this system, however, is much greater in the shorter distances. This metabolic pathway is one important component in swim performance. Typical sets that will develop this area are listed next:

1. 10 × 10 meters or yards on 1:00
2. 8 × 15 meters or yards on 1:15
3. 5 × 20 meters or yards with a dive on 1:30

Anaerobic Glycolysis Pathway

Another source of energy production in the muscle that can be maintained for longer periods of time is muscle glycogen. If the energy demand is relatively high, the muscle breaks down glycogen through anaerobic pathways. A by-product is produced during the breakdown of glycogen called lactic acid. The lactic acid accumulates in the muscle cells and can begin to inhibit further energy production and muscle contraction. The glycolytic pathway can produce relatively high amounts of energy for up to about two minutes. If continued work is necessary, energy must be generated through aerobic pathways.

Aerobic Pathway Training

When the activity lasts longer than one and one-half to two minutes, the aerobic pathways are used. Aerobic pathways use oxygen in the process to generate energy. Energy production can be maintained for long periods of time with this system; however, the intensity of the work must be reduced.

Have you ever purchased a new automobile and had the salesperson request that the first 2 to 3 thousand miles be driven at speeds less than 55 miles per hour? These "base miles" were driven at lower speeds for mechanical reasons. The car's engine needed a foundation before faster speeds could be obtained. We can apply this analogy to the human machine. To swim fast you need to swim "base miles" and those "miles" must be in the aerobic zone. Quantity and quality are not polar opposites when used to describe training. Terms that are more appropriate might be *volume* and *intensity*. The use of appropriate volume and intensity in a progressive manner during a training cycle allows for maximization of the training load. The term *aerobic* is often incorrectly associated with slow, easy swimming. Aerobic intensities range from very easy to very intense. Few athletes would consider an aerobic workout containing a 6,000-meter swim for time as an easy practice. Therefore, it is very important to remember that aerobic training is not merely slow swimming for hours.

Young athletes need a progressive program of aerobic training. They will respond to this style of training over time. To date, very little research suggests that young athletes are successful later in their career without a foundation of aerobic work. In fact, anecdotal evidence abounds supporting the benefits of a strong aerobic base in both children and adults. Sprinters such as Mark Spitz, Jonty Skinner, and Tom Jager trained and swam distance events (successfully) before they became world-class sprinters. An aerobic base must be pursued early in the swimmer's career, and it should be maintained throughout his or her entire career.

To enhance the concept of aerobic training, it appears that controversy exists in the area of how much and how often. Many groups such as runners, cyclists, and swimmers have used the concept of threshold or anaerobic threshold (AT) training, which causes the body to supply energy more efficiently using aerobic sources. A swimmer will be capable of maintaining faster paces without the negative effects associated with anaerobic metabolism. Assume a swimmer could improve the pace corresponding to his or her anaerobic threshold by 10 percent, and the swimmer in this case does not alter the pace at which he or she can swim anaerobically. If the aerobic contribution to an event occurs at the anaerboic threshold pace, the two-minute 200-meter freestyler before anaerboic threshold training (swim components: 61 percent aerobic; 39 percent anaerobic) would now be appreciably faster. This decrease in time is related to the changes in the anaerboic threshold velocity (more efficient aerobically). Data from other sports support the use of anaerboic threshold training. To estimate an athlete's anaerboic threshold, have the individual swim continuously for approximately 30 minutes and divide the time by the total amount swum to obtain a 100-meter or yard average pace. (See chapter 5 and the appendixes for more information on this.) Use this as a guide for training either above, below, or at the anaerboic threshold. The exact benefits that will occur vary from athlete to athlete. Anaerboic threshold training, however, is one viable method to enhance a swimmer's aerobic ability.

Daily Planning

The day-to-day challenges of training design are normally the most important to the coaching community. Coaches should ask themselves how they can maximize each practice to give their swimmers the greatest chance for success. Following are some factors coaches need to consider when designing practices.

Practices are and should be a preparation for competition! Everything that is done in practice should lead a swimmer on a progression from training to competition. During the competition phase, anything that could happen in a race should already have been experienced in a practice setting. Progression also needs to occur within the longitudinal training plan. Changes in workout intensity, frequency, and volume should progress throughout the period of development over the course of a season and the year, as well as the career of the swimmer.

Interval training is the most common form of training. A practice is designed based on using a number of training sets that involve time intervals as send-offs for given distances. Set design is only limited to the imagination of the coach. Given the multidimensional aspect of this topic it is important to break this factor down further. The following few paragraphs review some basic aspects related to different types of set construction that a coach may use in every practice.

❖ To prepare the body for hard work, every practice should begin with a warm-up. The warm-up should prepare the swimmer in both a physiological and psychological sense. The duration of the warm-up could be very short and comprise only one set or a little bit longer and use a few sets.

❖ It is very common for a coach to have a main set for a workout. This set should be the primary focus of the practice and may require a high level of mental concentration and physical fatigue. It can be structured in many different ways but should always work toward the goal(s) that are being developed.

❖ A coach should always end every practice with some type of a cool-down period. The cool-down is in the form of active recovery that will facilitate the repair of physiological stress resulting from the practice. Not only does the cool-down aid in recovery from the current workout, but it also is vital in preparing the swimmer for the next workout. Although the cool-down is something that is often overlooked, it is important if the swimmer is to reach his or her full potential. Just as a cool-down is important in practice, it may be even more important in a competition setting.

It has become quite popular for athletes to do some type of cross-training. The most common type of cross-training for swimmers involves dryland work. Typical forms might include calisthenics, body-weight exercises, weightlifting, running, medicine ball work, using rubber tubing, and possibly even biking. It is very important for coaches to consider how the dryland training can be structured to improve swimming performance.

Tracking Improvement

A coach and an athlete need to have measurement points along the way to measure improvement based on the training plan. The obvious first tracking area is the athlete's performance in swim meets. The key question should be "Is the athlete's performance in swim meets consistent with expectations based on the training load?" A coach may make necessary adjustments to the training based on performance in a meet. Meet performance, however, is not the only way for a coach to track improvement.

Another essential element to tracking improvement is the use of test sets in practice. Test sets should be designed to test the various energy systems that a coach is trying to overload and adapt. Run test sets every couple of weeks, and be sure that they are run in the same consistent manner every time. Over time, results from test sets will give the coach and the athlete a more accurate picture of overall development than swim meet performance.

four

Biomechanics

Jane Cappaert

Athlete Progression Levels 1–5

In the beginning levels (1 through 5) of the Progressions for Athlete Development, improvements in a swimmer's performance depend on two factors: skill acquisition and growth. Growth is a natural benefit that an athlete will have as they continue swimming over the period of a few years. But growth will only improve a swimmer's ability to a certain degree. The continued success of a swimmer will remain if the basic principles of stroke technique are learned by the swimmer and reinforced by the coach. This chapter is designed to provide coaches with the background knowledge of the principles and why they are important to success in swimming. This section for levels 1 through 5 focuses mainly on developing basic principles for each stroke.

Streamlining and Sculling

Two hydrodynamic principles seem to apply across the board to swimming the four strokes for fun and competition. These principles are streamlining and sculling. Mastering these two principles generally leads to successful swimming.

Streamlining

The first thing that comes to mind when a coach mentions streamlining is the "torpedo" position with the arms stretched out above the head on both sides. The torpedo position should be used during starts and turns when the body is completely submerged underwater. The head placement is the most critical to minimizing the water drag. The most streamlined position is with the ears between the arms. Just the slight motion of lifting the head toward the spine doubles the drag from the water. Often the head will lift before breaking the water surface after starting or turning, even at the elite level. This doubling of the drag can add up to precious tenths of seconds, especially during races of short duration. The drag is not dramatically affected if the head is placed forward toward the chest.

Sculling

The phrase, "feel for the water," is used by coaches to describe a swimmer who has natural ability with strong skill potential. It seems difficult to teach a "feel for the water," but it is easy to recognize. The best way to develop this kind of sensitivity is through sculling drills. Sculling is the basis of each stroke. A good sculler has a good chance of becoming a proficient swimmer. In teaching freestyle and butterfly, coaches and instructors typically demonstrate the strokes as sweeping S-shaped patterns. Relative to the water, however, there is very little backward motion involved in any of the pulling patterns. Using a simplistic model, the hand in freestyle enters the water and sweeps outward, inward, and outward again. Although the freestyle pulling pattern involves downward and upward motions, each pull is mainly a scull.

A sculling motion is the most propulsive way to swim for several reasons. As the hand pushes back against the water during a pull, the water begins moving toward the feet. Moving water does not allow forceful pushes. The sideways sweeping motion of sculling allows the hand to push off "still water." In addition, the sculling motions use lift forces as well as drag forces for propulsion. The use of the lift force helps to direct the total force from the hands forward, adding to propulsion.

Because of these reasons, both streamlining and sculling cannot be overemphasized in workouts and practice. These principles should be the foundation of your program.

Water Drag and Resistance

Water drag affects a swimmer in different ways. One way is through the impact of water with a swimmer and the subsequent flow of water around the body (form drag). Another way is through water turbulence and waves that are created by moving water (wave drag). A third way is through water sticking to a swimmer's suit or skin and creating resistance (friction drag). These three drag components all have a negative effect on swimming performance and should be reduced whenever possible.

Form Drag

Form drag is resistance from the water that is dependent upon body position. The more horizontal the body position becomes in the water, the more form drag decreases. Swimmers should try to stay up near the water surface (especially with the hips) during all strokes. A slanted body position will enlarge the frontal surface area in the vertical direction and increase the form drag. Extreme lateral swaying in the water is another example of increasing the form drag due to greater frontal surface area.

Wave Drag

Wave drag is caused by turbulence at the water surface created by the moving swimmer. Wave drag will rebound off the sides and bottom of a pool, which is why deeper pools are generally "faster" pools. The dissipation of the wave drag off the bottom of deep pools is much greater than for shallow pools. Two and three lane lines per lane are used at high-level competitions to disperse the wave drag.

Frictional Drag

Frictional drag originates from the contact of the skin and hair with the water. Swimmers shave body hair before important meets to minimize the effects of frictional drag. The actual drag-reducing benefits from shaving are still being questioned. Some researchers have suggested that shaving the hair from the skin reduces the frictional drag. The resistance caused by form and wave drag, however, are undoubtedly much more significant than the frictional drag.

Individual Strokes

Body position, arm action, kicking action, and timing for each of the four strokes are discussed in the following sections. Following these basic descriptions, some basic drills are explained to help teach the stroke. These are followed by a number of drills that can be used to correct common stroke faults or errors.

Freestyle

Body Position

A straight body position in freestyle should be maintained at all times, along the vertical line, side view, and the horizontal line, top view. During the stroke the body rotates along an axis that extends through the spine. The head is still facing with the eyes generally looking toward the bottom of the pool unless the swimmer is breathing in and out. The stroke initiates with hip rotation and starts on one side and rotates to the opposite side.

Arm Action

The arm stroke begins with an entry of the hand. As the arm extends, a swimmer should begin to apply pressure to the hand and forearm down and backward. The arm then accelerates through the length of the stroke. The recovery of the stroke begins with the elbow, and the high elbow position is maintained throughout the recovery phase.

Kicking Action

The kick initiates at the hip and extends through the toes. A whip-like motion of the knees and ankles is important for maximum propulsion (up to 30% of the total propulsion). The kick may vary in tempo from the preferable faster six-beat kick to a slower two- or four-beat kick. The kick should be maintained throughout the stroke cycle.

Timing

The arms, legs, and breathing are coordinated with the body roll. The entry arm extends as the opposite arm completes the final phase of the pull. This allows the body to rotate to the side where it achieves the most streamlined position. The kick is continuous throughout the body roll and has an even cadence. Breathing occurs as the lead arm enters the water and the opposite arm finishes the stroke. The head should remain flat in the water with the lower ear and goggle in the water.

Drills

Flutter Kicking Drills

The teaching progression for freestyle should emphasize kicking. A six-beat kick is recommended because it adds to propulsion more than does the two-beat kick. Swimmers can kick down the length of the pool using a six-beat kick with the head up and the hands sculling or using a breaststroke pull out in front of their bodies. An important part of properly performing this drill is plantar flexion at the ankle (pointing the toes) and medial rotation.

Flutter kicking while rotated on the side is a natural drill progression that also begins to highlight body roll. This drill can be done with both arms at the swimmer's side or with one arm stretched out in front and the other resting on the upside of the body. Swimmers can kick down the length of the pool with their stomachs facing one side of the wall and then come back on the other side, or they can rotate from side to side after every six kicks.

Sculling Drills

Sculling drills emphasize the sweeping motions of all the strokes and help to develop "feel for the water." Sculling in the prone position (head up) with the hands out in front is a drill that swimmers should use to work on all of the strokes. The hands make sweeping figure-eight motions. This same drill can be done on the back with the hands at the swimmer's sides. Vertical sculling in the deep end of the pool is another variation of this drill. Weights can be attached to the advanced scullers during the vertical sculling. All of these drills help the swimmer to learn the most effective way to move through the water through trial and error.

Stroke Correction

Improving Body Roll

The 12-12 drill aids in body roll. The swimmer kicks on one side with one arm extended for 12 counts and then does one stroke to the opposite side. This drill emphasizes the timing of the breathing, a strong finish, and a good body roll.

Dropped Elbows During Entry

The Hand, Wrist, Elbow drill helps to correct dropped elbows. The swimmer begins walking in the water. He or she executes the arm strokes for each arm and pays close attention to the high elbow position and the streamlined hand entry. Picking up speed, the swimmer falls forward and begins swimming full freestyle strokes with the high elbow entry position.

Excessive Crossover of the Arms

Crossing too far over the midline of the body (more than six inches) can cause a poor transition between the insweep and the finish of the pull. The Head-Up Freestyle drill helps to correct this pattern. The swimmer travels across the pool doing freestyle with the head raised out of the water during the entire stroke cycle. This head-up position limits shoulder and hip rotation, making it more difficult to cross over the midline of the body.

Dropped Elbows During the Recovery

The Fingertip Drag drill can help develop high elbows during the recovery. The swimmer raises the elbows high on the recovery and drags the fingertips along the surface of the water next to the body. The elbows must be high to accomplish the fingertip drag.

Late Breathing

The Single Arm Freestyle drill will correct the timing of the breathing. The head begins to rotate laterally to the opposite side as one hand enters the water. This occurs as a natural roll with the shoulders. The head rolls back into the water as the pull finishes.

Backstroke

Body Position

A straight body position in the backstroke should be maintained at all times along the vertical line, side view, and the horizontal line, top view. During the stroke, the body rotates along an axis that extends through the spine. The head rests at the lower ear level. The stroke initiates on one side and rotates to the opposite side.

Arm Action

The arm stroke begins with an entry of the hand, with the little finger entering first. As the arm extends, the swimmer begins to apply pressure to the hand and forearm down, out, and backward. The arm bends underwater. The arm then accelerates through the length of the stroke. The recovery of the stroke begins with the thumb. The arm is recovered toward the sky. When the arm is over the shoulder, the body rotates the arm in the water with the little finger entering first.

Kicking Action

The kick begins from the hip and extends through the toes. The knees should remain underwater at all times and the ankles should plantar flex so that the toes are pointed for maximum propulsion. The kick is a fast, even-tempo six-beat kick. The kick is maintained throughout the stroke.

© Allsport

Timing

The arms and legs are coordinated with the body roll. The entry arm extends as the opposite arm completes the final phase of the pull. This allows the body to rotate to the side where it achieves the most streamlined position. The kick is continuous throughout the body roll and has an even cadence. Breathing occurs as the lead arm enters the water and the opposite arm finishes the stroke. The head should remain still.

Drills

Flutter Kicking

Flutter kicking on the back with the body in a streamlined position (arms overhead) is an important way to start the backstroke. The knees should bend through a 60-degree range of motion during the kick.

Sculling Drills

Sculling drills should be emphasized in each of the strokes including backstroke (for details on sculling drills see the freestyle section).

Stroke Correction

Improving Body Roll

Lack of proper body roll can cause improper hand position (not leading with the little finger) as it enters the water. Without the correct hand positioning, the hand does not have the proper pitch for the catch phase. In addition, swimmers will not be able to drive the hand down very deep during the catch phase without proper roll. The Six and Six drill can help to correct this problem. During this drill the swimmer rotates from the hip to one side and lifts the opposite shoulder to the chin. The swimmer remains in that position for six counts. Following the count of six, the swimmer takes one complete stroke to the opposite side and remains rolled to that side for six counts again.

Proper Hand Entry Position

The Wrist Rotation drill will help correct the problem of swimmers entering the water thumb first rather than little finger first. This drill is accomplished by swimming one stroke at a time.

While the right arm is stroking, the left arm remains down at the side. The thumb exits the water first on the straight-arm recovery. As the arm progresses through the recovery, the swimmer pauses with the arm pointed at the ceiling (12:00 position) and rotates the wrist 180 degrees. The swimmer then continues the recovery and concentrates on the hand entering the water with the little finger leading.

Crossed Over Arm Entries

The Double Arm drill is particularly useful for swimmers who have a tendency to cross over on the entry. Both arms pull and recover together throughout the stroke. Because of the double arm pull, it is almost impossible for swimmers to cross over during the entry. This drill, however, should not be used extensively because it does not allow for body roll.

Slow Turnover

During the Spin drill, swimmers rotate their arms through the water as fast as they can. This drill is particularly useful in increasing the turnover rate of the stroke. It is also helpful for swimmers who have the tendency to stop at the finish of the pull. The swimmer should be well warmed up to avoid ballistic injury.

Breaststroke

Body Position

The stroke begins with the swimmer floating flat on the stomach, with the hips and shoulders maintaining a horizontal line at the surface. The chin should be slightly forward. The swimmer's head should stay connected to the upper body through an imaginary line through the spine—the head and chest move up as one unit. The arms should be extended shoulder width apart.

Kicking Action

Beginning from a streamlined position, the heels lift toward the swimmer's buttocks. The knees should be close (about shoulder width apart), with the heels further apart during the propulsive phase of the kick. The feet turn out, with the bottom of the feet facing backward, once they reach maximum bend. The bottom of the feet rotate inward in a sculling type motion during the kick back, down, and around. The lower legs accelerate backward, outside the knees, and together in one motion. Heel speed during the kick is important.

Arm Action

Beginning with the arms extended in front of the shoulders in a streamlined position, the arms begin to press wide until they are outside the shoulders. They make a smooth transition from outsweep, to insweep, to recovery and return to the starting position. The elbows should remain higher than the hands throughout the insweep or power phase. The arms sweep in under the chin and not backward.

Timing

The stroke begins from a streamlined position, with the hands together and the arms extended. The swimmer begins the stroke by pressing the arms out, maintaining a flat body position. As the arms make their transition from outsweep to insweep, the body should lift and the breath should be taken. The legs begin the kick as the arms start their recovery. At the finish of the recovery the kick accelerates backward. The arms should remain fully extended until the completion of the kick, when the legs are pressed together.

Drills

Breaststroke Kick With Hands in Front

This drill allows the swimmer to glide in a streamlined body position following the completion of each kick. Have swimmers count the number of kicks it takes to cross the pool. As they become better at kicking the number of kicks across the pool should decrease.

Breaststroke Kick on the Back

This drill is effective for those swimmers who tend to draw the knees up under the body. Breaststroke Kick on the Back forces the swimmer to drop the heels down while keeping the knees below the surface of the water with no splash. This then allows the legs to be in the proper position for the propulsive phase of the kick.

Sculling Drills

Sculling drills must be emphasized for each stroke. For details on sculling drills, see the Freestyle section.

Stroke Correction

Pause After the Insweep Phase

For swimmers who pause their arm strokes just after the insweep phase, the Breaststroke Arms with a Flutter Kick drill will help correct the problem with the pull. Because of the flutter kick there is no pause in the stroke. This drill facilitates quicker arm strokes, eliminates the pause at the ribs after the insweep, and works on the timing of the stroke.

Kick Too Wide

To correct a wide kick, swimmers should perform the breaststroke kick with a pull buoy between their thighs. This drill constrains the width of the knees and forces the swimmer to lift the heels during the kick.

Scissor Kick

The Garbage Bag drill helps correct the kick of a swimmer who is not able to turn both feet outward. The drill gives the swimmer the feel for the correct position and power of the kick. The swimmer lies down on the deck on a wet garbage bag. The coach places the swimmer's feet in the correct position in preparation for the kick. The hands of the coach are placed on the swimmer's feet. The coach then encourages the swimmer to kick. As the swimmer kicks, he or she slides across the wet plastic. This drill can also be done in the water. Another swimmer or the coach can stand in the water with his or her hands holding the swimmer's feet in the proper position. Again, the swimmer kicks and glides through the water.

Developing the Insweep and Undulation Motion

The Rope drill will help swimmers improve the insweep phase during the pull. Stretch a rope or stretch cord approximately 12 to 20 inches over the surface of the water (depending on the age and strength of the swimmer). Swimmers must accelerate through the insweep phase of the pull for their head to touch the rope. This strong insweep causes the shoulders to clear the water. Swimmers should also remember to continue the arm pull through to the recovery.

Another drill to develop the undulation motion is Swimming Breaststroke Arms with a Dolphin Kick. This drill is also an ideal way for breaststrokers with knee problems to work on their breaststroke timing.

Timing

The Three-One drill in which the swimmer does three pulls then one kick or three kicks followed by one pull can help with timing. Another useful drill is doing the breaststroke pull with either a dolphin or a freestyle kick.

Butterfly

Body Position

The swimmer begins the stroke by floating flat on the stomach, with the hips and shoulders at the surface. The chin should be slightly forward, and the head should stay connected to the upper body. The arms are extended shoulder width apart.

Arm Action

The arms enter the water shoulder width apart with the thumbs in first. The arms slowly press out and down, building speed. When the hands reach the widest part of the entry/catch phase of the stroke, the swimmer turns the palms in and accelerates the arms in toward the midline of the body (insweep phase) and then back out toward the hips (outsweep/finish phase). During the recovery, the arms swing low and forward over the water back to the entry position.

Leg Action

The butterfly requires a dolphin kick. The dolphin kick undulates from the hip to the knees to the ankles and through the feet, with the knees and feet close together. Usually two kicks are done per arm pull, although some world-class swimmers do just one.

Timing

Coordination of all body movement is crucial for a relaxed smooth stroke. The stroke begins with the arms extended; the first kick occurs at the entry. The arms sweep out and down and accelerate toward the hips. As the hands pass under the chin, the feet begin the upbeat of the second kick. As the hands finish moving toward the hip, the legs finish the downbeat of the second kick. The breath occurs during the power phase of the arms by pushing the chin forward and lifting the head slightly. The head returns to the water just before the arms enter.

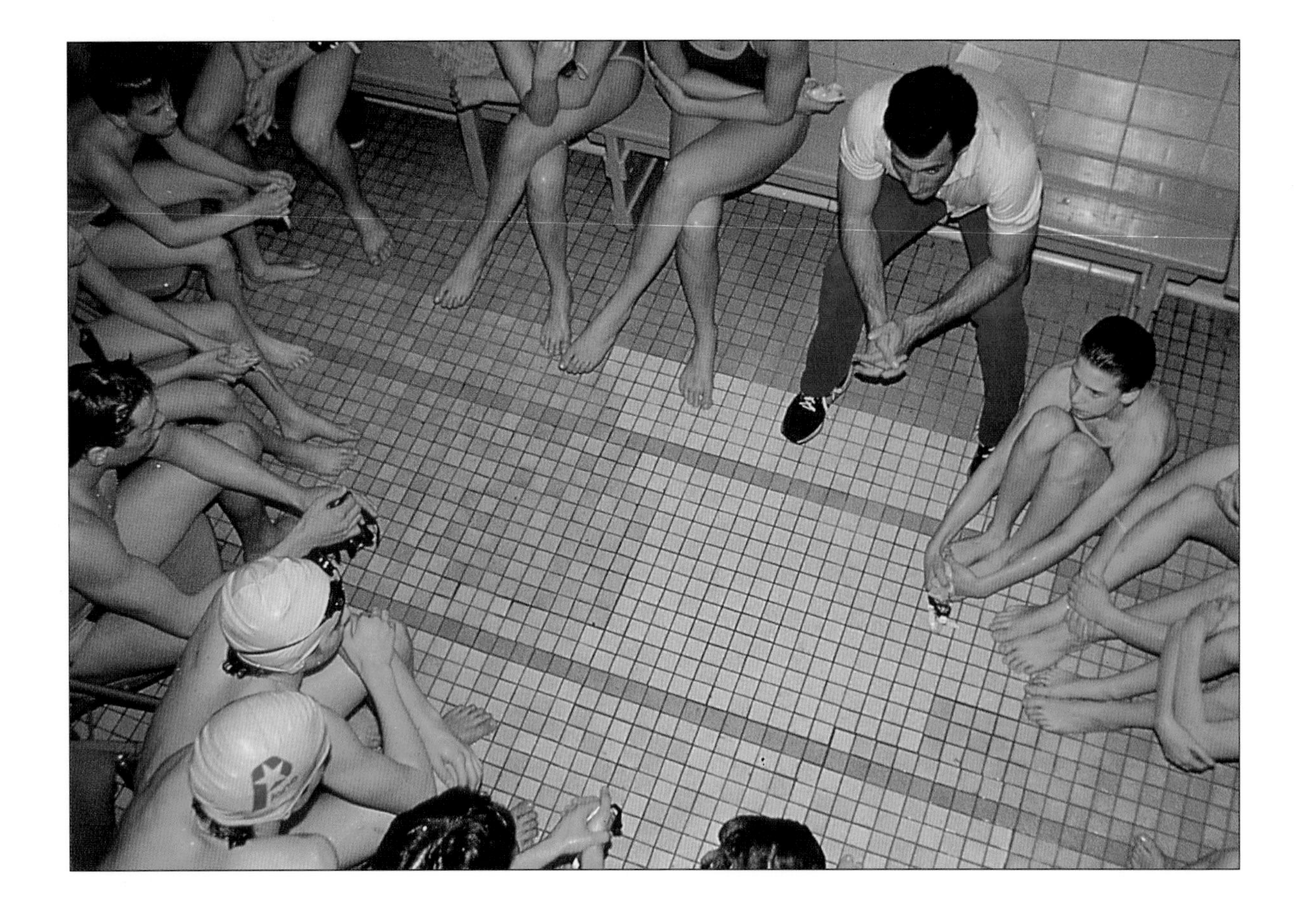

Drills

Underwater Dolphin Kick on the Back

The first drill is the Underwater Dolphin Kick on the Back. The main purpose of this drill is to teach the swimmer the importance of both the up and down movement of the kick. The swimmer pushes off the wall on the back and performs the dolphin kick (see section on butterfly leg action on page 57) across the pool.

Dolphin Kick Streamlined

The next drill is also a kicking drill. The swimmer does a dolphin kick on the stomach or on the side in a streamlined position, concentrating on keeping the hips up. The swimmer should lift the head at the appropriate time for a quick breath, or a small breaststroke pull may be used to breathe. The kick should not stop while the breath is taken.

Sculling Drills

Sculling drills should be emphasized to promote the sweeping motions of all the strokes. For details on sculling drills, see the Freestyle section.

Stroke Correction

Developing the Undulation Motion

Dolphin kicking while a swimmer is on the side of the body helps to emphasize both the upward and downward motion of the kick equally. The kick should originate from the hips rather than from the entire body. Vertical kicking in deep water with the hands at the side is also a good position from which the coach can observe the swimmer's undulation from the side, front, or back.

Improper Timing

The Crawlfin drill helps with the timing of the butterfly stroke. Swimmers swim freestyle with the arms and dolphin kick with the legs. The breath occurs naturally as it would in freestyle.

Developing the Catch Phase

Sometimes young swimmers will pull straight backward with the hands in a very narrow position. The Catch Scull drill helps to develop feel for the water and teaches the swimmer the importance of the catch phase. The swimmer does three to four sculls with the hands in the entry position (out in front of the body) followed by three full strokes, emphasizing the catch and scull outward after the entry.

Monitoring Stroke Technique

The easiest way to monitor stroke technique improvements is to use distance per stroke. Although athletes can swim the same velocities with very different stroke rates and distances per stroke, the key to elite swimming seems to be a long distance per stroke with a slower stroke rate. This finding has been shown in the swimming research literature and continues to be true in the United States. Figures 4.1 to 4.3 illustrate this trend. Figure 4.1 shows the changes in midpool swimming velocity of the top eight male competitors at the USA Swimming Olympic Team Trials from 1976 to 1996. Figures 4.2 and 4.3 display changes in stroke rate and distance per stroke cycle, respectively. Although not shown, the data for female swimmers are similar. In almost every event, swimmers are swimming faster today than they were 20 years ago using longer distance per stroke and a slower stroke rate.

To monitor an athlete, you can simply count (or have the athlete count) the number of strokes taken per length of the pool. Stroke technique improvement would be achieved when the athlete is swimming faster for the same number of strokes or swimming the same pace with fewer strokes. See the section that follows on how to monitor distance per stroke more specifically.

Here are some articles containing more information on swimming velocity, distance per stroke, and stroke rate:

Craig, A.B., Jr., and D.R. Pendergast. 1979. "Relationships of Stroke Rate, Distance per Stroke and Velocity in Competitive Swimming." *Medicine and Science in Sport* 11:278-83.

Craig, A.B., Jr., P.L. Skehan, J.A. Pawelczyk, and W.L. Boomer. 1985. "Velocity, Stroke Rate, and Distance per Stroke During Elite Swimming Competition." *Medicine and Science in Sports and Exercise* 17:625-34.

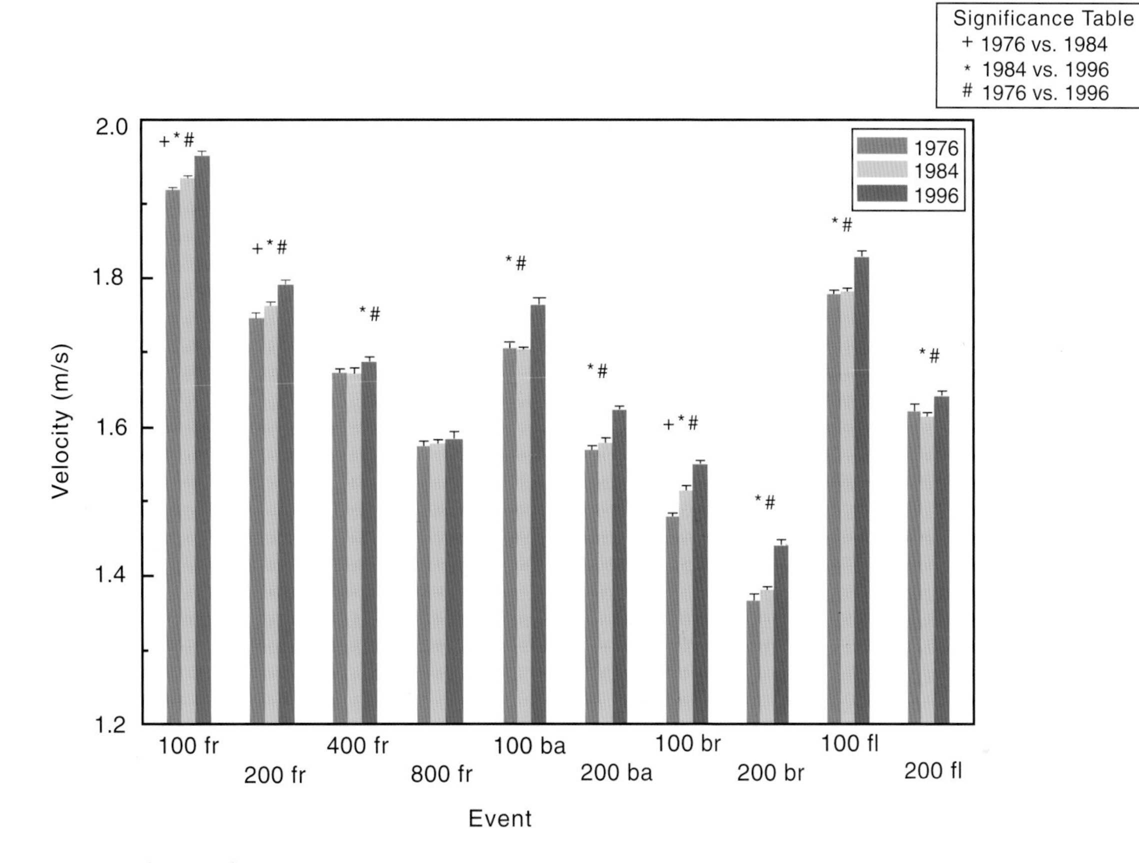

Figure 4.1 Velocity analysis—men's events.

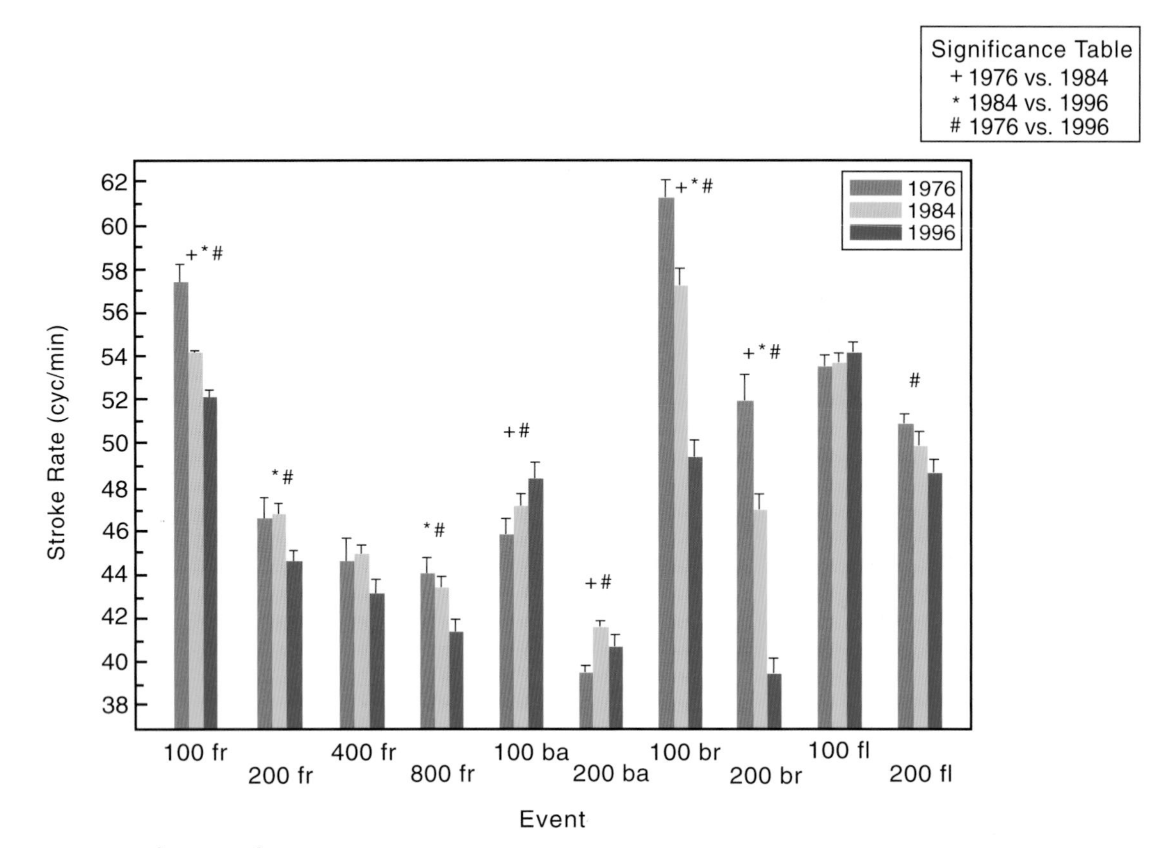

Figure 4.2 Stroke rate analysis—men's events.

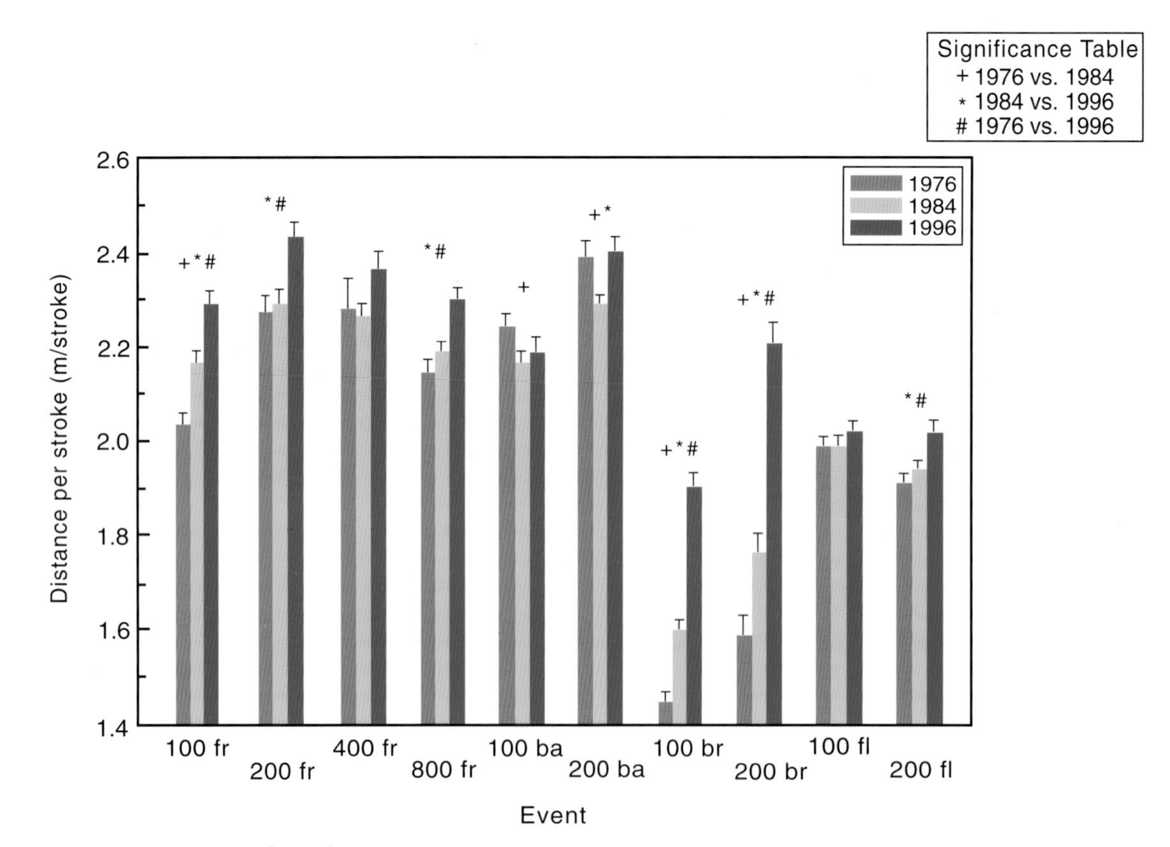

Figure 4.3 Distance per stroke analysis—men's events.

Read the following for further information on monitoring distance per stroke:

To monitor distance per stroke more specifically, follow these basic steps. Mark off a certain distance in the midpool section of the pool, for example, 10 meters or 10 yards. Within this midpool section, record the time that it takes to swim through that distance. In addition, record the time for five complete stroke cycles within the midpool section (right-hand entry to right-hand entry). You may get results that look like this:

Time to complete 10 meters = 6.3 seconds

Time for 5 stroke cycles = 5.1 seconds

To calculate Stroke Rate and Distance per Stroke:

1. Calculate Swim Midpool Velocity (Vel):

   Vel = the distance completed divided by the time it took to complete the distance

   Vel = 10 meters/6.3 seconds = 1.59 meters/second
2. Calculate Stroke Rate (SR):

   SR = the number of cycles divided by the time it took to complete the cycles

   SR = 5 cycles/5.1 seconds = 0.98 cycles/second

   (On the race data sheets, the stroke rate is in seconds/cycle)

   To obtain Cycles per Minute:

   0.98 cycles/second × 60 seconds/minute = 58.8 cycles/minute
3. Calculate Distance per Stroke (D/S):

   D/S = Vel (usually expressed as meters/second) ÷
   SR (usually expressed as cycles/second)

   D/S = (1.59 meters/second) / (0.98 cycles/second) = 1.62 meters/cycle

You may also calculate stroke rate and distance per stroke in a 25-yard pool. Multiply your velocity in yards/second and distance per stroke in yards/stroke by 0.91 (one yard = 0.91 meters) to get velocity in meters/second and distance per stroke in meters/stroke. Once you have calculated these numbers for your athletes, you can evaluate where your swimmer(s) need to make progress. For example, if a female 100-meter backstroker's velocity is slower than the finalists in the women's 100-meter backstroke, and she has comparable D/S, you can focus her training on slightly increasing stroke rate while maintaining distance per stroke to increase swimming velocity.

Advanced Principles for Levels 6 Through 8

At the advanced levels (6 through 8) of the Progressions for Athlete Development, improvements in an athlete's performance can be more difficult to achieve. Generally speaking, these athletes are at a high performance level, and improvements are not as dramatic as they are with developing athletes. The biomechanical section of the athlete progressions in levels 6 through 8 focus mainly on improving speed through a focus on distance per stroke. This section of the Progressions for Coach Development is designed to provide coaches with insight into how to improve technique and, therefore, distance per stroke.

This section is technical and may possibly be difficult to understand at times. However, understanding the specific details (as learned through scientific research) of how to maximize propulsion and minimize resistance gives a coach the tools to evaluate the individual technique of his or her own athletes. This will not be a simple formula for swimming fast. The idea in this section is to get you to think about how technique variables interact with each other and emphasize the important phases of each stroke.

Background

Pulling Pattern Propulsion

Drag force is also used for propulsion during the pulling pattern and the kick. As the arm pulls back against the water, the water, by reaction, pushes the arm and the body forward. The drag force is one component of this reaction force, and its line of action is opposite the direction of the water flow.

The Italian physicist Bernoulli first described the lift component of fluid forces. Bernoulli's principle expresses the relationship between flow velocity and the created pressure differential on two sides of an airfoil. In swimming, differences in the water flow around the hand during the pulling pattern create the lift force.

The amount of lift force that is present during a pull is dependent upon the shape of the object and the angle of attack or pitch of the object. An airplane wing generates high amounts of lift with very little pitch (10 degrees), whereas a hand in swimming develops high amounts of lift with 30 to 55 degrees of pitch.

Pulling Pattern Forces

As the hand pushes against the water during swimming, the water provides lift and drag forces that propel the swimmer through the water. These forces can be indirectly calculated using fluid force lift and drag equations. The amount of force produced by the hand at any time during the stroke cycle is dependent upon the hand orientation and its speed or velocity.

The forces exerted by the hand are more complicated because the hand does not remain in a fixed position as would a blade on a propeller. Also the shape of the hand is not uniform. Water flows differently over the thumb than it does over the wrist. The coefficients of lift and drag represent these different flow characteristics and vary depending upon the origin of the water flow across the hand. Because the pulling pattern is mainly a sculling motion with angles of pitch midway between 0 and 90 degrees, the lift force is especially important in producing propulsion.

Lift and drag forces can be calculated using the following equations:

Lift Force = $^1/_2$ × (density of water) × (velocity)^2 × (coefficient of lift) × (frontal surface area)

or

$$L = {}^1/_2\, pV^2C_LA$$

Drag Force = $^1/_2$ × (density of water) × (velocity)^2 × (coefficient of drag) × (frontal surface area)

or

$$D = {}^1/_2\, pV^2C_DA$$

Explanation of Propulsive Force Curve Figures

Each stroke is presented next with accompanying force curve figures that progress through the stroke and highlight phases of propulsion. The series of figures includes six frames of the force curves and arm views. Beside each of the hand force curves are side, front, and bottom views of the arm as it moves through the stroke. The calculated lift, drag, and total forces are shown on the hand. The red line extending from the back of the hand represents the drag force, the yellow line represents the lift force, and the black line represents the total force. The frame numbers are in the upper right hand corner of each box (e.g., the first row of figures listed on page 64 is from frame 10 and is marked "f10").

On the left side of the figure is a series of force graphs. The uppermost curve on the force graph (in yellow) represents the total force produced by the pulling pattern. The lower curve (in black and red) quantifies how much of the total force is either "resistance" (any force below zero, shown in red) or "propulsion" (any force above zero, shown in black). The white vertical line in the force graph represents the stage of the stroke that is represented in the side, front, and bottom views to the right of the force curve. Usually during hand entry, some of the total force produced is negative, or resistive, and acts to slow the body. During the sculls much of the total force produced is propulsive force and acts to propel the body through the water.

Ideally, we would like all of the total force to be propulsive, although this is extremely difficult to achieve. Our working premise is to minimize the resistive force to the body and to maximize the propulsive force. The following technique recommendations are based on this premise.

Strokes

The next section discusses the four strokes in detail. For each stroke, the phases of the pulling pattern in which arm propulsion is maximized is discussed. Additionally, different methods for streamlining to reduce resistance are presented.

Freestyle

Maximizing Pulling Pattern Propulsion

Typically, the forces generated by the hand during the entry into the water are resistive (f10, f20). The key to this phase therefore is streamlining. The time period of this phase and the length of the hand extension helps to determine the amount of body roll and the amount of resistive forces. Emphasizing body roll during the entry causes the hand to stretch further out in front of the body, resulting in an increase in resistive forces. Other swimmers who emphasize high turnover rates typically begin their catch phase quickly after hand entry. Although they are met with fewer resistive forces, they usually do not have as much body roll.

Small amounts of propulsive force and total force are generated during the end of the catch phase of the pulling pattern (f35). Most of the force from the hand is directed upward, which may help the swimmer stay higher in the water.

The insweep phase is the first major phase of propulsive force (f44). Freestylers typically display a bimodal force application pattern. The first burst of force occurs during the insweep phase. The amount of propulsive force is highly dependent upon the lift force that is generated by the sweeping or sculling motion of the hand. The average hand angle of pitch during the insweep is 30.4, plus or minus 4.6 degrees, for men and 30.5, plus or minus 5.9 degrees, for women.

Between the insweep and finish phases, a transition phase occurs where the forces acting on the hand decrease slightly (f52). This transition phase occurs because the hand must change directions from sweeping in toward the body to sweeping away from the body. To achieve this change in direction hand speed must slow down causing a decrease in the propulsive forces.

The finish phase is usually the most propulsive phase of the pulling pattern due to increasing hand velocity (f62). The hand velocity during the finish phase averages 2.1, plus or minus 0.3 meters per second for elite level male athletes and 2.0, plus or minus 0.4 meters per second for elite female athletes. To maximize the propulsion of the finish phase forces, the wrist hyperextends to maximize the propulsive component of the forces acting on the hand.

Minimizing Resistance

Body position has an effect on streamlining, and body roll in the freestyle has streamlining benefits. By rolling the body, the frontal surface area (head on view) is reduced. Body roll helps the body mimic the shape of the bottom of a boat (V-shaped) rather than the flat bottom of a barge. The V shape of a boat slices through the water with less drag than would the bottom of a barge.

Report for Freestyle (file FREE):

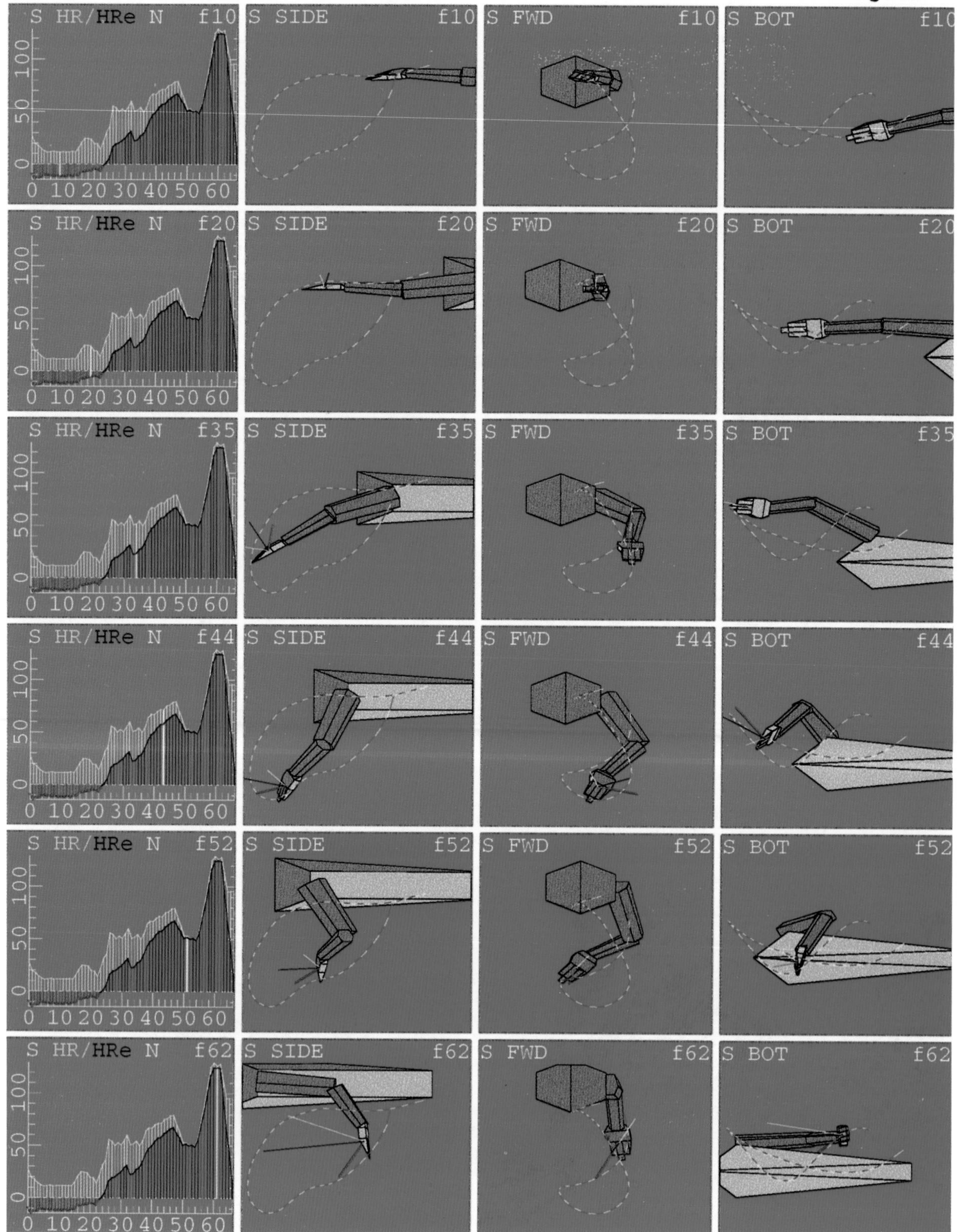

Backstroke

Maximizing Pulling Pattern Propulsion

The entry into the water can have very little resistance especially if the little finger enters first (f2). Because the arm is fully extended upon entry, there is little stretching forward underwater and therefore minimal resistance. The resistive forces are higher during the entry if the swimmer slaps the water with the back of the hand. The main purpose of the catch (f2) is to set the hand in position for the pull phases of the stroke (upsweep and downsweep). The entry into the water, however, can be slightly propulsive.

The upsweep is the most propulsive phase of the pulling pattern for most swimmers (f9). The average angle of attack of the hand for elite swimmers differs between men and women during this phase (36.6, plus or minus 6.6 degrees, and 49.1, plus or minus 7.7 degrees, respectively).

As the pull continues through the downsweep, additional propulsive force is generated (f14, f16). For some elite swimmers the downsweep can be the most propulsive phase as hand velocity typically reaches its peak. Another function of the forces that are generated during the downsweep is to assist in hip roll. Most swimmers have an upward component of the forces from the hand during this phase. This upward force helps to raise the hip on the same side as the downsweeping hand upward as well.

The finish phase begins at the end of the downsweep, with the hand being slightly deeper than the hip and right next to the body (f20). The function of this phase is to exit the hand out of the water in as streamlined a position as possible. This is best done with the thumb leading. By exiting out of the water in this fashion, no propulsive forces arise, only resistive forces.

The finish and exit out of the water can be done with a different and distinct pattern. Some swimmers end the downsweep phase very deep (6 to 10 inches deeper) and wide to the body (10 inches from body). The finish phase then consists of a sweep or a scull up and toward the body, which can be propulsive. This type of pulling pattern seems to occur naturally in some backstrokers. Although the benefit of this pattern is extra propulsion during the finish, the disadvantage is that these sweeping motions introduce sideways swaying of the hips and shoulders that may decrease the efficiency of the whole body. The swimmers who use this sweep during the finish most often develop the motion naturally rather than being taught.

Minimizing Resistance

As in freestyle stroking, body roll has streamlining benefits. By rolling both the shoulders and the hips symmetrically the swimmer can reduce frontal surface area. Again, body roll helps the body mimic the shape of the bottom of a boat (V-shaped) rather than the flat bottom of a barge. The V shape of a boat slices through the water with less drag than does the flat bottom of a barge.

Breaststroke

Maximizing Pulling Pattern Propulsion

The outsweep phase is generally not highly propulsive. Its main function is to set the hands in proper position for the insweep phase. Swimmers who sweep upward as well as outward and flex the wrists are able to create small amounts of propulsion during the end of the outsweep phase (f4).

The insweep phase is the most propulsive phase of the pulling pattern. This phase is usually only approximately 50 percent propulsive, however (f10, f13). This discrepancy is due to the fact that the insweep phase is more of a lateral scull with very little backward pull. This insweep motion comes closer to pure sculling than any other swimming motion. Therefore, it relies heavily on the lift force for propulsion, and the pitch of the hands is approximately 40 to 50 degrees with respect to the line of motion of the hand. Some swimmers can increase the propulsive component of the insweep to 60 percent, but 100 percent propulsion is rare.

The recovery phase is never propulsive, and the goal of recovery is to minimize water resistance by streamlining the hand position. The largest amounts of resistance occur at the beginning of the recovery phase (f21). This is because the hands are not yet in a streamlined position. Once the hands are streamlined, the resistance

Report for Backstroke (file BACKA): Backstroke Page 2

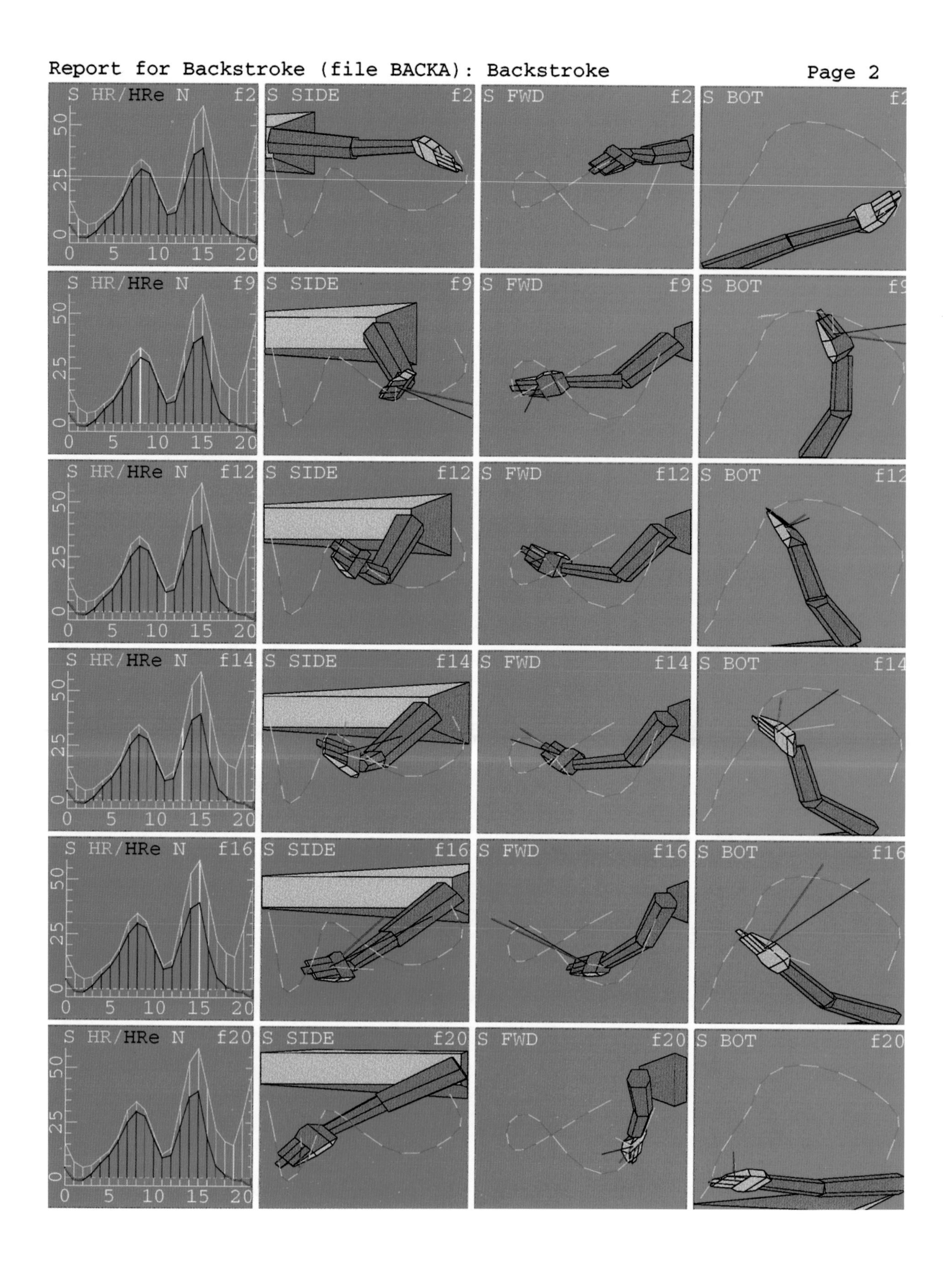

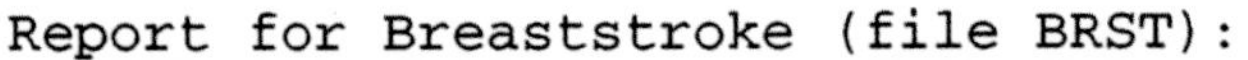
Report for Breaststroke (file BRST):

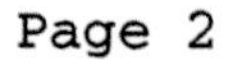
Page 2

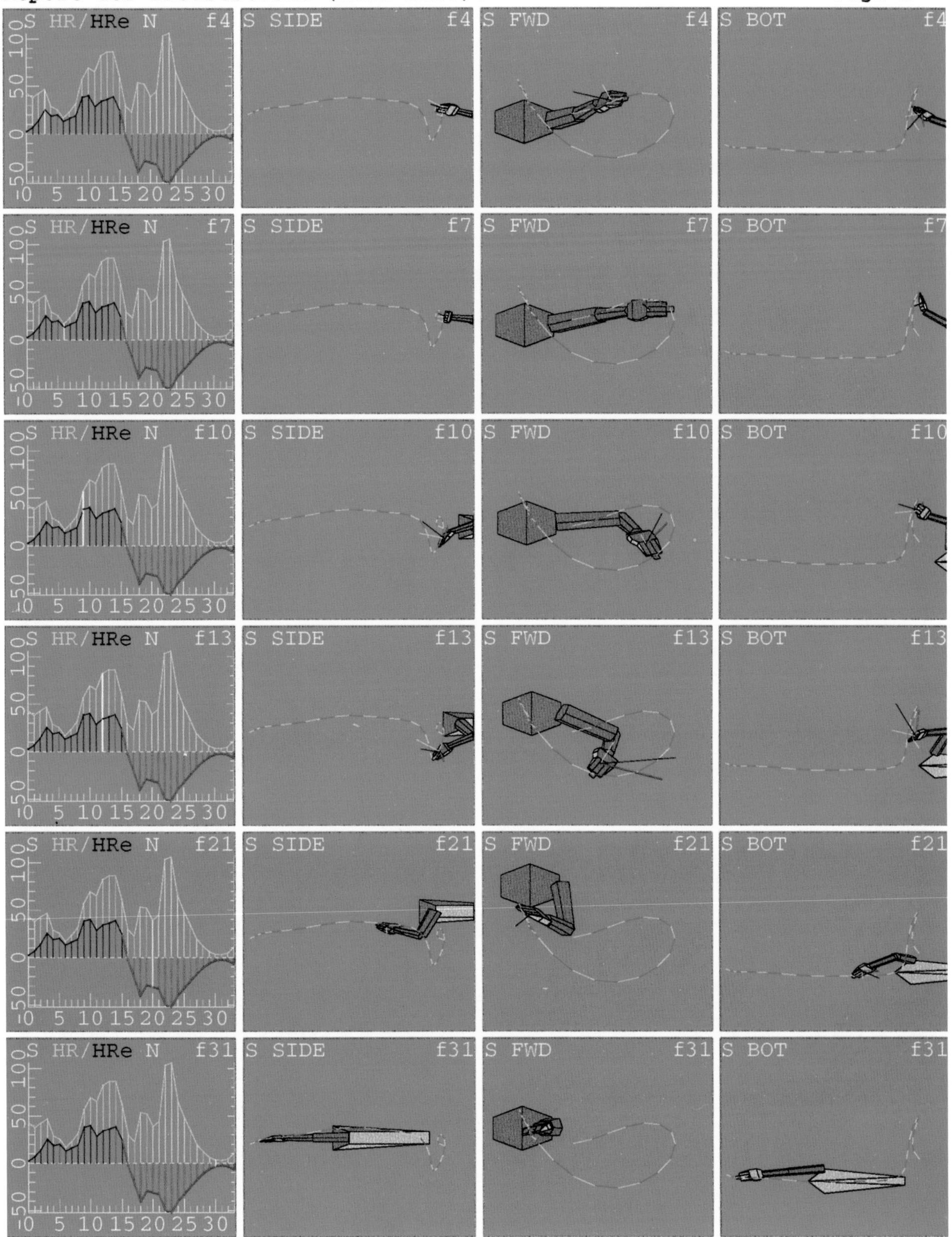

from the water can be minimal (f31). Several hand positions are streamlined: palms together, palms facing downward, and palms facing upward. There seems to be no difference between these hand positions in terms of water resistance. Some swimmers recover their hands slightly above the water or at the water surface. This recovery can be useful in reducing water drag as long as the whole body position is maintained. Often when swimmers attempt the over water recovery, the angle of the trunk increases greatly. This increase in trunk angle usually causes an increase in body drag. Therefore, it seems that the over water hand recovery is difficult to execute properly. A large increase in the trunk angle would negate the benefits of such a recovery.

Minimizing Resistance

In the breaststroke the angle of the trunk during the breath also has implications for streamlining. Raising the shoulders straight up out of the water (high trunk angle) also forces the knees to drop slightly during the leg recovery. This position creates large amounts of drag due to the increase in frontal surface area.

Butterfly

Maximizing Pulling Pattern Propulsion

The propulsive forces generated by the hand during the entry into the water on the butterfly are low and sometimes resistive or negative (f4). Because the arms enter the water fairly extended, the resistive forces from the water are usually minimal.

Small amounts of propulsive force can be generated during the end of the catch (f8), but this phase mainly sets the hands in position for the more propulsive insweep phase. Most of the force from the hands is directed upward, which may help the swimmer stay up in the water (f8).

The insweep phase is the first phase of propulsion (f12). Butterfliers usually show bimodal force applications where the first burst of force occurs during the insweep phase. The lift force used during this sculling insweep phase creates the propulsion. The hand pitch during the insweep averages 44.8, plus or minus 13.3 degrees, and 32.9, plus or minus 7.9 degrees, for men and women, respectively.

A transition occurs between the insweep and finish phases, which causes the forces to decrease slightly (f15). This transition phase occurs because the hands must change directions from sculling inward to sculling outward. To achieve this change in direction, hand velocity decreases, and, therefore, the forces decrease.

The finish phase is usually the most propulsive phase of the pulling pattern due to high hand velocities (1.93, plus or minus 0.62 meters per second, and 1.53, plus or minus 0.38 meters per second, for men and women, respectively, see f18). To maximize the propulsive potential of this phase, swimmers should hyperextend the wrists, keeping the backs of the hands facing forward (f20). This hand position uses lift and drag almost equally to direct the forces forward.

Minimizing Resistance

As with the breaststroke, minimizing the trunk angle helps to keep the stroke more streamlined by reducing the frontal surface area. Hand entries in the water should be as streamlined as possible, and the head should stay down as it enters the water.

Report for Butterfly (file FLY):

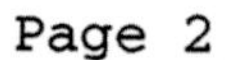

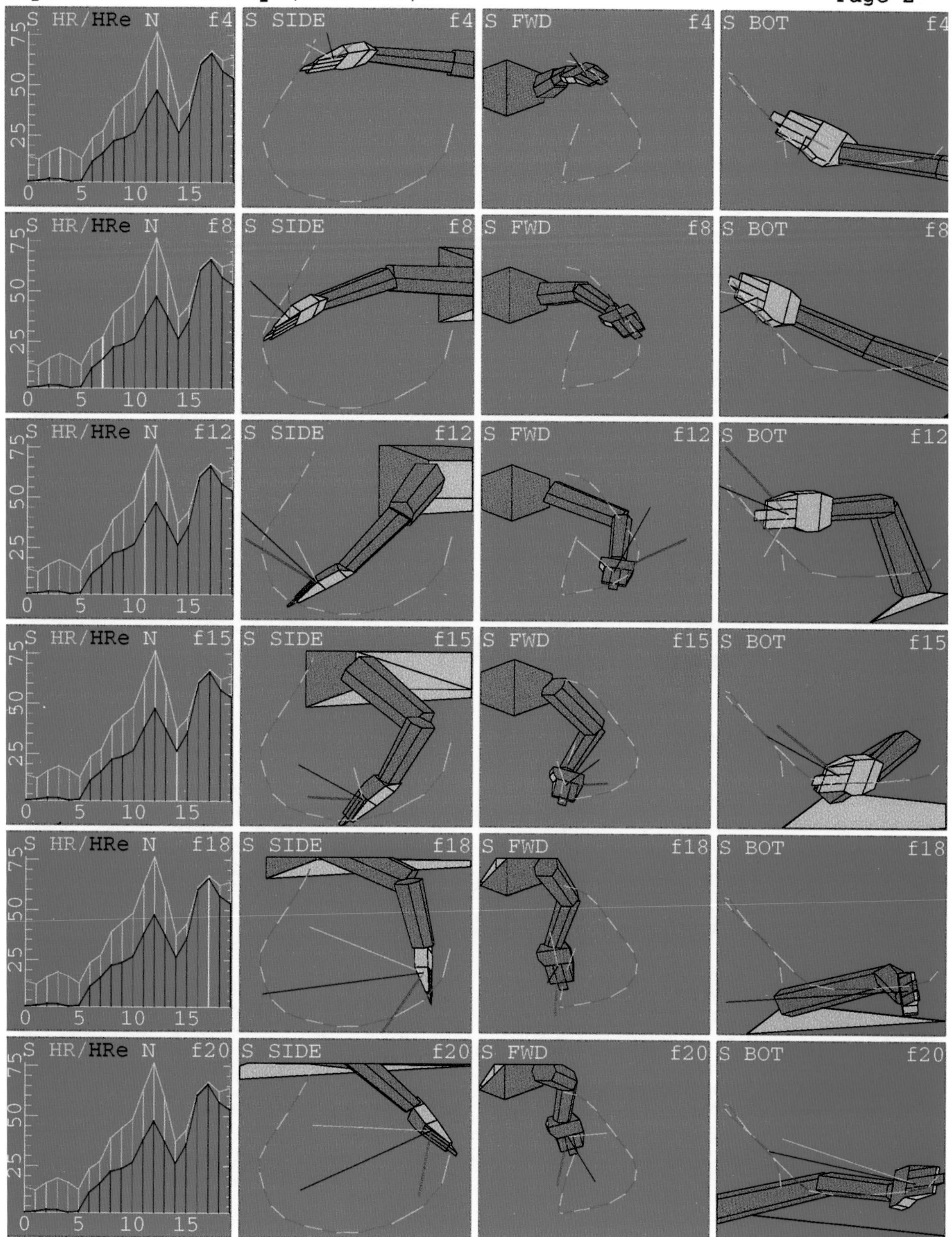

five

Physiology

Jaci Van Heest, PhD

The goal of training is to cause changes in muscles, the circulatory system, and the metabolic pathways. The adaptations are quantitative and/or qualitative. Quantitative changes are seen as an increase in the amount of a structure or substance. A quantitative change could be the increase in the number of capillaries that supply blood to a skeletal muscle that can occur with aerobic training. Qualitative changes are adaptations in the characteristics of the body or its components. An example of a qualitative change would be the adaptations that occur in neuromuscular communications that occur in prepubescent children training for swimming on dry land. Many factors influence the training adaptations that occur such as age, gender, and ethnicity. An example of this would be the differences in aerobic ability between males and females. These types of factors must be considered when developing metabolic pathways and the associated organ systems in the body.

Metabolism can be divided into two major categories—aerobic and anaerobic. The energy demand of the swimmer (based on the activity) dictates the metabolic pathway(s) utilized. Fuel stores must also be considered when planning training programs that cause adaptations in metabolism. Stored glycogen (carbohydrate) and triglycerides (fat) within the muscle are two important fuel reservoirs. High-energy phosphates (adenosine triphosphate and creatine phosphate) are also stored within the muscle and provide an immediate energy source. Dietary consumption of fats, carbohydrates, and proteins provide the building blocks for stored fuels within the body. It is important to recognize that appropriate dietary habits are critical for athletes to perform to their maximum potential both in training and competition.

Aerobic Endurance

Aerobic endurance is the foundation of performing physical work. Aerobic metabolism or pathways generate energy from fuels within the body (fats and carbohydrates) using oxygen in the processes (see figure 5.1). The aerobic pathways can produce energy for extended periods of time (large capacity) when the intensity of the exercise is low. The relationship between intensity of exercise and duration or time of the activity is inverse like a "teeter-totter." For example, when the intensity is high the duration of the work performed is short. This is an example of anaerobic work that is high intensity and can only be maintained for short periods of time.

You can develop a swimmer's aerobic potential or aerobic endurance by exposing the swimmer to workouts that are longer in duration at a somewhat lower intensity. Repeat distances may only consist of one pool length for a young athlete (levels 1 and 2), and the focus of the work should be on skill acquisition. Continuous swimming with good technique enhances aerobic endurance at these ability levels.

As swimming skill develops in levels 3 through 7, a T30 or threshold set can be used to monitor adaptations in aerobic endurance. The protocols for both a T30 and a threshold test set are described next.

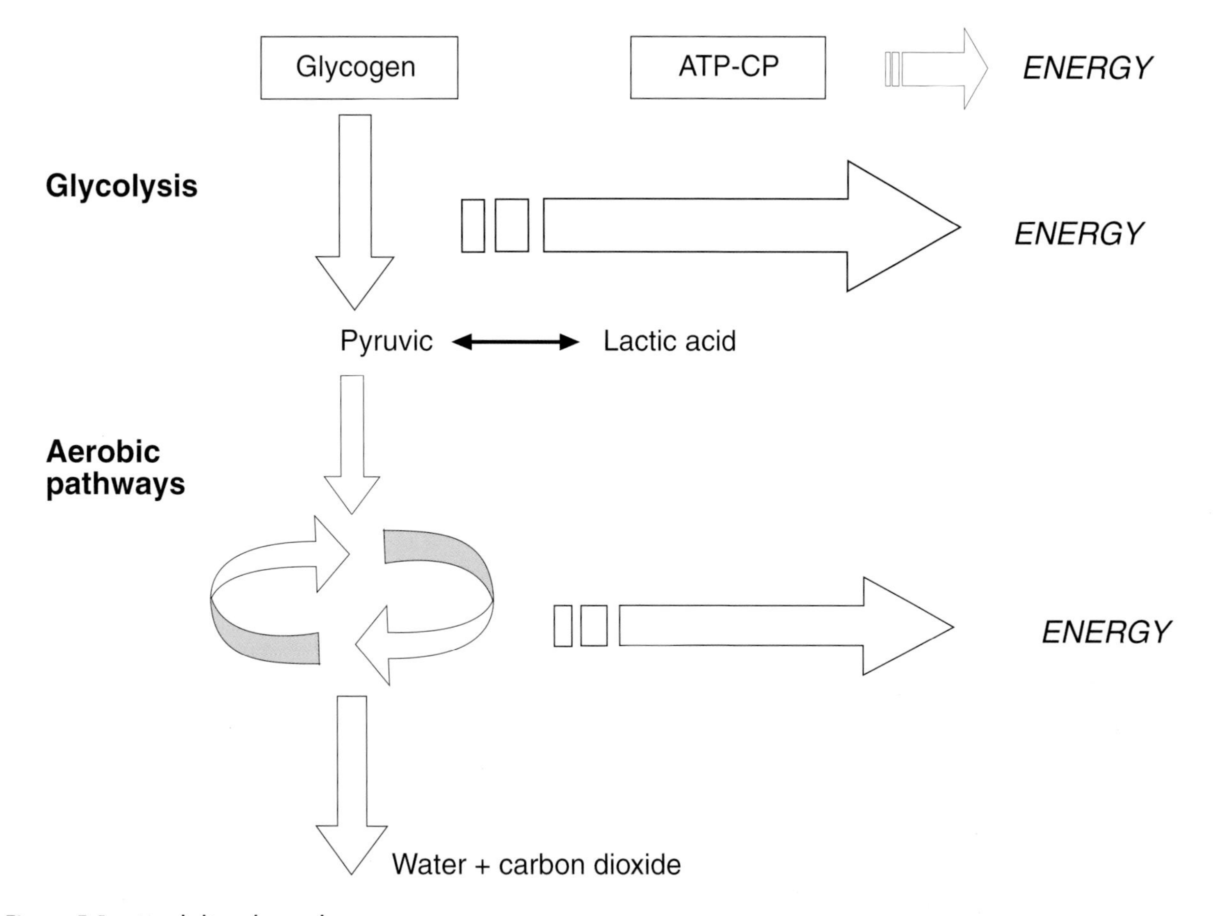

Figure 5.1 Metabolic pathways that generate energy.

T30 or Timed 3,000 Swim

Olbrecht, Madsen, Mader, Liesen, and Hollmann (1985) developed a method to test the validity of training sets in predicting the four-millimolar threshold pace for swimmers. They found that the average pace during a 30-minute swim (at the maximal effort possible) was similar to the 4mM threshold pace. The 30-minute swim test has been named the *T30*. The remainder of this section illustrates the protocol for a T30 test.

1. Measure the distance the swimmer covers in a 30-minute continuous swim. The swim must be the *maximal* effort that the athlete can perform. Maintaining an even pace is also a critical component of this swim test.
2. Calculate the average pace for 100 yards or meters

Descending 6 × 200 Meters/Yards Curve Test Set for Lactate Threshold

Many coaches and athletes use lactate testing to determine the efficiency of training programs, predict performance, prescribe training intensities, identify overtraining, and prevent injury or illness. This type of testing allows for the determination of a lactate threshold. Lactate threshold is defined as the point at which blood lactate begins to accumulate above resting levels during exercise of increasing intensity. A significant shift toward anaerobic metabolism occurs at this point. The ability to exercise at a high intensity without accumulating lactate is advantageous to swimmers because lactate accumulation contributes to fatigue. Lactate testing is one of many scientific tools available to develop the potential of swimmers. Incorporation of heart rate into this test allows for a field tool that can be used by coaches to monitor training. The following list describes the protocol for performing the 6 × 200 meters/yards test to determine an athlete's lactate threshold.

1. The athlete performs a standard warm-up designed by the coach. This same warm-up should be used for each of the testing times throughout the season
2. The athlete swims 200 meters/yards six times descending by approximately five seconds each, repeating to an all out maximal effort on the last repeat. The interval for each repeat is five minutes. Each effort should be approximately five seconds faster than the previous swim.
3. The coach measures heart rate and stroke rate for each swim. Fifteen-second heart rate counts should be taken, or an electronic device like a heart rate monitor should be used. (Sample heart rate data are given in table 5.1.)
4. After the final swim a recovery heart rate is taken immediately and then again in 45 and then 90 seconds.
5. Plots of the heart rate versus time or velocity should be made (see figure 5.2).

The data illustrated in table 5.1 are typical for swimmers performing this protocol. While this table does include blood lactate levels, this may be too complex for most coaches to perform. The same general information can be obtained by charting heart rates. Additional information such as recovery heart rates can also be placed in either a table or figure format. To evaluate biomechanical efficiency, a coach may also want to consider tracking the stroke rate and distance per stroke during the third 50 of each test repeat. It is important to evaluate both the mechanical and physiological components of this test over the course of the season.

Figure 5.2 is an example of two consecutive curve tests. The time 2 results show that the athlete performed poorly on the second trial compared to the first testing session (time 1). The shift of the curve for time 2 up and to the left is indicative of the maladaptation in this swimmer. The swimmer's poor performance could be related to sickness, additional stress due to an emotional or psychological cause, or other physical stress factors. It is important for the coach to be aware of the elements in each athlete's life to best understand his or her response to the test protocols.

Key Terms

Aerobic endurance—The ability to perform steady state swimming at the highest possible intensity. Dictated by the athlete's ability to take in, transport, and utilize oxygen and the ability to delay the onset of accumulation of lactic acid in the blood.

Aerobic metabolism—Occurs in the presence of oxygen; aerobic metabolism utilizes oxygen to produce energy for muscular contraction.

Table 5.1 Results From a Lactate/Heart Rate Profile

Swim number	Time (min:sec)	Average 100m (sec)	Heart rate (bpm)	Lactate (mMol)
1	2:35	77.5	144	1.5
2	2:23	71.5	158	2.3
3	2:19	69.5	166	3.6
4	2:15	67.5	175	4.7
5	2:10	65.0	185	7.4
6	2:05	62.5	191	11.4

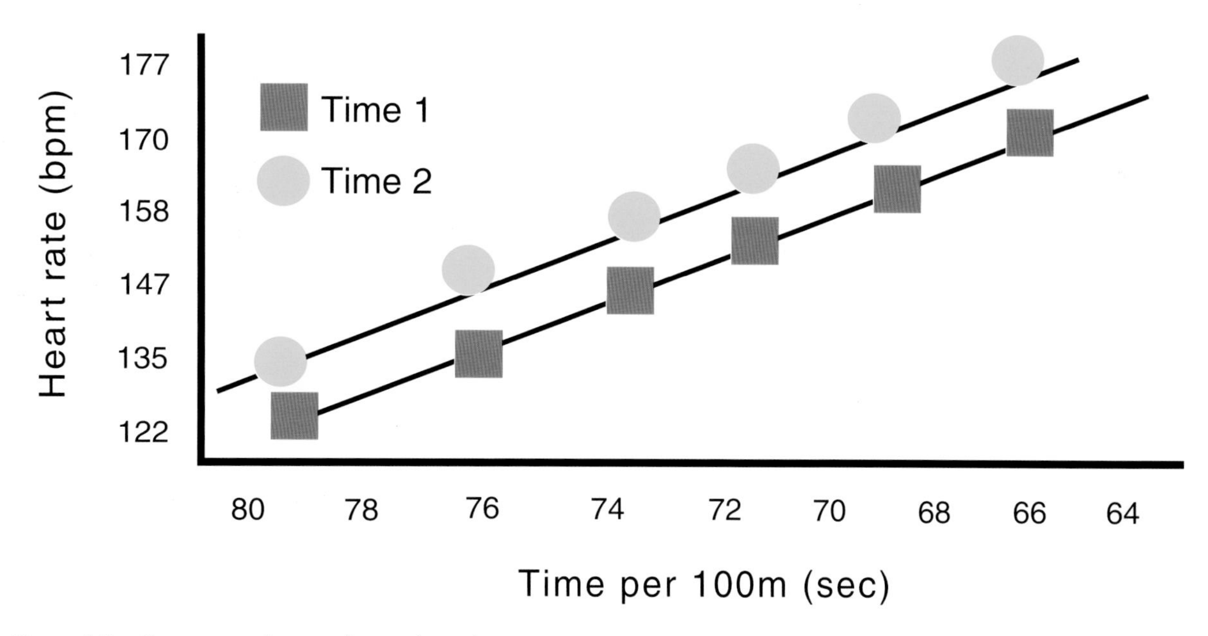

Figure 5.2 Heart rate and swim velocity relationship.

Exercise duration—The length of time of the repeat or total swim.

Exercise intensity—The pace of the swim.

Threshold—Occurs when aerobic metabolism can no longer supply all of the energy needed to maintain the intensity of activity. Also called anaerobic threshold. Blood lactate accumulation in the muscle is greater than its removal, resulting in a net accumulation of lactate in the muscle and blood.

Muscular Strength and Endurance

Swimmers need both muscular strength and endurance to perform optimally. Strength is defined as the maximal force a muscle can generate. Muscular endurance is the ability to lift a load repeatedly. Strength and endurance are different, and the swimming requirements for each depend on many factors. One example of how they are important is in injury prevention, especially in the shoulder and knee.

The development of muscular strength increases at the time of puberty and beyond. The properties of muscle are influenced by changes in hormones during and following the period of puberty. Prior to puberty, the increases in muscular strength and/or endurance are associated with adaptations in neuromuscular communications, which allow the nerves and muscles to function more effectively as a unit.

Puberty onset is a process during which time the athlete "evolves" into a biologically mature adult. Boys and girls do not typically mature at the same rates; boys are delayed in comparison to the girls. Typical onset of puberty is 12 years of age for girls and 15 years for boys. These ages, however, are merely guides or averages. You must consider the biological maturity of your athletes when using dryland weight training to increase muscular strength and/or endurance.

Sit-ups, push-ups, and pull-ups require a specific amount of strength to raise the body weight against gravity. Repeating these tasks either until fatigue or within a specific time frame is a test of muscular endurance for swimmers in levels 5 through 7.

Key Terms

Muscular endurance—The ability to lift a load repeatedly.

Muscular strength—The maximum amount of force that can be generated in a single effort.

Puberty—The period in life during which an individual becomes functionally capable of reproduction.

Sprint Capacity ATP-CP System

Production of energy is the goal of metabolism. Energy is needed to enable muscles to contract. The demand for energy is related to the intensity of the work placed on the body. If the energy demand is high, the body must generate energy very rapidly. To accomplish this task, muscle cells contain immediately accessible fuel stores—ATP and CP. ATP (adenosine triphosphate) and CP (creatine phosphate) are energy-rich fuel stores that are contained within the muscle cells. The supply of these fuels is limited; therefore, the high-intensity work can be maintained only for relatively short periods of time (less than 10 seconds). Work beyond this point must be maintained by other energy-producing pathways.

The ATP-CP system provides some energy for all swim distances. The portion of the total energy output by this system, however, is much greater in the shorter distance swims. This metabolic pathway is one important component in swim performance.

Sprint training sets (e.g., 12 × 25 meters/yards on 3:00 minutes) can serve to both test and train this metabolic pathway and are appropriate for levels 5 through 7 in the Progressions for Athlete Development. Other "spot-check" sets can be used (e.g., 2 × 25 meters/yards at maximal effort from a push-off start) throughout the season to assess sprint ability.

Key Terms

ATP—Adenosine triphosphate is a high-energy compound. ATP supplies energy to the muscle and serves in other body functions.

CP—Creatine phosphate is an energy-rich compound that backs up ATP in providing energy to the muscles.

Lactate Tolerance

Lactate tolerance is the ability to withstand the pain and fatiguing effects of lactic acid accumulation in the muscles during very fast swimming. This ability is probably related to motivation, psychological pain tolerance, and muscle buffer capacity. Training for lactate tolerance is defined as an SP1 pace in the USA Swimming training categories scheme (see appendix A). The purpose of this form of training is to increase muscle buffer capacity and improve aerobic power.

Characteristics of a lactate tolerance set would include a swim that lasts for a duration of 3 to 12 minutes, using a repeat distance of 50 to 200 meters/yards. The work to rest interval would be from 1:1 to 1:2, and the intensity is approximately 90 to 95 percent of the swimmer's best 100 pace. Lactate values in this training range would be between 10 and 20 millimolar.

Here is a sample set to train lactate tolerance:

12 × 100 on 2:30

Intensity is the pace of the second 100 split in best 200 time.

Key Term

Lactic acid—A by-product of anaerobic glycolysis.

References

Olbrecht, J., Madsen, O., Mader, A., Liesen, H., Hollmann, W. 1985. "Relationship between swimming velocity and lactic acid concentration during continuous and intermittent training exercises." *International Journal of Sports Medicine* 6:74-77.

six

Character Development and Life Skills

Suzie Tuffey, PhD

Broadly speaking, outside of a national character and an educated society, there are few things more important to a country's growth and well-being than competitive athletics. If it is a cliché to say athletics build character as well as muscle, then I subscribe to the cliché.
—Gerald Ford, 1977

People often say that sport builds character and that, through the sport experience, participants learn skills that they can transfer to other endeavors. But little evidence has been found to support this blanket statement (Sage 1998; Shields and Bredemeier 1995). Sport participation alone does not guarantee positive character development or life skills development. What can be stated is that sport participation has the *potential* to influence the development of an individual, both positively and negatively. Sport can be viewed as offering the opportunity to practice "good" behavior if structured appropriately, modeled, and reinforced by coaches.

When asked why they coach, coaches often talk about how they enjoy working with kids, teaching about life through sport, instilling values, or having a hand in making someone a better person. (Often, coaches make no mention of producing winners as a reason for coaching.) Coaches need to take a step back and assess whether or not these coaching values, principles, and motivations are reflected in their thoughts, actions, and the structure of the swimming environment. Positive character and value development do not occur automatically; such development only occurs with forethought and purposefulness on the part of coaches. Coaches need to identify how they are going to influence their swimmers positively and how they are going to structure sport as an opportunity for athletes to learn and practice positive behaviors.

The type of influence sport participation has on an individual seems to be influenced by the sport environment, the behavior of role models, and the content of what is communicated and emphasized, to name a few factors, all of which coaches have a hand in controlling.

Sage (1998) suggests that

> little serious thought seems to be given to the well-known principle that whatever attitudes, values, and beliefs that will be acquired by young athletes will be strongly related to the values, actions, and morality that are displayed, admired, and rewarded in the social environment in which sport participation takes place (17).

Championship Behavior and Accountability

An overriding theme regarding the development of championship behavior (sportsmanship) is respect—respect for teammates, for coaches, for parents, and for competitors. "To respect something is to value it and treat it as worthy in its own right" (Clifford and Feezel 1997).

Athletes should be expected to demonstrate progressive levels of respect for others; these expectations should be clearly communicated and modeled by the coach.

Athletes show respect for the coach by paying attention when the coach is communicating and by attempting to implement coach recommendations (level 1).

Athletes demonstrate respect for their teammates by treating them as they themselves would want to be treated. The athlete is able to step outside of him- or herself and view a situation from another perspective and then use this information when making decisions about appropriate behaviors (levels 1 and 2).

Athletes understand and accept team rules as well as the consequences for disobeying team rules. They view themselves as one member of a large team that functions best when all abide by team guidelines (level 1).

The coach should be a role model of sportsmanlike behaviors:

> As a coach you must constantly keep in mind that your actions do, in fact, speak louder than your words. No matter what you say, what you do will have an effect on your players. You must do everything you can to show your players what it means to be a good sport by treating opposing players and coaches, officials, team members, and the sport in which you participate with respect. (Clifford and Feezell 1997, 100)

Coaches should seek opportunities to reinforce positive behaviors by using "teachable moments" (i.e., teaching a value within the context of a real-life situation) to demonstrate appropriate and inappropriate behaviors. View these teachable moments as opportunities to begin to instill the development of sportsmanlike thoughts and behaviors.

Although there is no all-inclusive list of behaviors that constitute sportsmanship–championship behavior, it is important to discuss with athletes the importance of being sportsmanlike and to provide examples of such behavior. The long-term objective is to make sportsmanlike behaviors a habit.

Coaches should establish team rules and customs that promote desired behaviors with clear guidelines regarding punishment for misbehavior. Athletes understand these desired sportsmanlike behaviors as well as the consequences for displaying unsportsmanlike behaviors (level 2). In addition, the athlete understands the importance of talking to the coach before and after races and works to communicate effectively at these times (level 2).

Athletes are expected to understand and demonstrate increasing levels of sportsmanlike behaviors; increased respect for coaches, teammates, and competitors is also expected. The athlete progresses from being told how to behave in specific situations to using reasoning to make his or her own decisions about appropriate behaviors in given situations (level 3).

Ask your athletes questions to encourage them to reason through the question and make their own judgment or decision. As a coach you are also a teacher, and good teaching involves asking appropriate and thought-provoking questions rather than force feeding athletes the answers (Clifford and Feezel 1997).

The athlete respects his or her competitors. This respect is demonstrated, in part, by knowing competitors' names and by viewing them as a positive influence in the athlete's quest for excellence (as opposed to viewing competitors as the enemy). The athlete realizes that the challenge of swimming against an opponent will enhance the athlete's own performance (level 4).

Athletes understand and accept the responsibility for their competition preparation and performance. They understand further the importance of controlling what they can to enhance performance and of not allowing the uncontrollables to negatively affect performance (level 5).

Although athletes may not seek out the role of being a leader, it is a position in which they often find themselves. Athletes are aware of their leadership position and understand how they can positively influence the behavior of others. Athletes understand and accept that effective leadership comes with the responsibility of being a positive role model to others. They recognize the need not only to do good things and demonstrate sportsmanlike behavior but also to guide and influence others toward demonstrating such behavior (level 6).

The athlete is unselfish in giving his or her time to help the younger swimmers. He or she not only demonstrates positive behaviors but also gives hands-on help to others (level 7).

With maturity and experience, athletes accept increasing responsibility for their training. Although athletes want and accept advice, input, and help from coaches, they recognize that they themselves are ultimately held accountable for their training.

The athlete understands and helps develop his or her seasonal, yearly, and even quadrennial planning. He or she is accountable to the plan (levels 7 and 8).

The athlete recognizes that his or her leadership responsibilities extend beyond leading within his or her team or club to being a spokesperson for swimming to the public. Part of this responsibility involves communicating with the media and attending autograph sessions and other activities that tie to representing themselves and the sport (level 8).

Work Ethic and Self-Discipline

In general, the athlete should take increasing responsibility for demonstrating appropriate practice behavior and should progress from needing external motivation to train hard to being self-motivated and internally driven. The coach can enhance this progression by establishing a supportive environment, by communicating expectations clearly, and by modeling self-discipline and a strong work ethic.

Initially, self-discipline is reflected in positive practice behaviors such as showing up to practice on time, being responsible for any swim equipment the athlete uses, obeying pool and team rules, and paying attention to the coach during instruction. The coach should communicate and reinforce expectations of appropriate practice behaviors (level 1).

Work ethic and self-discipline are further developed in the athlete who swims the sets correctly (i.e., starts and finishes at the wall, doesn't walk on the bottom, leaves interval on time) without being monitored by the coach (level 2). Appropriate behavior, regardless of whether the coach is watching, demonstrates internalization of discipline instead of the discipline being imposed on the athlete from an external force.

The athlete is committed to the sport and to his or her team and demonstrates this commitment by attending practice regularly and being intense and focused in practice (level 3). The coach can foster athletes' commitment and motivation by helping them to clearly define individual and team goals and strategies to achieve these goals.

A strong work ethic is internalized such that dedicated, persistent behavior is demonstrated regardless of what teammates are doing. Furthermore, athletes resist the tendency toward "social loafing," where individuals tend to exert less effort in a group than when alone or when under the coach's eye. Swimmers understand the importance of challenging oneself on a daily basis and not allowing oneself to back off intensity (level 3).

Athletes demonstrate self-discipline in competition as well—showing up on time and being prepared to race. Although athletes may not always race well, they strive to always give the race their best effort (level 3).

The athlete progresses from being disciplined and hard working because of external forces to being self-disciplined because of an understanding that practice behaviors affect meet performance and the achievement of individual goals (level 4). The athlete recognizes the direct relationship between practice effort and race performance.

The athlete demonstrates self-discipline by resisting the negative behavior of teammates and not allowing others to have an adverse affect on his or her behavior. Instead, he or she is able to make an independent, reasoned decision regarding appropriate behavior and is able to cope with negative peer pressure(level 4). Such behavior, like any behaviors, is strengthened when reinforced and encouraged by significant others.

The athlete uses a variety of coping strategies to deal with pressure from parents and peers. Coping strategies for the athlete may include some of the following (level 5):

- ❖ Associates with a supportive network of athletes
- ❖ Clearly identifies and commits to individual goals and strategies to achieve goals
- ❖ Recognizes his or her inability to control others' expectations
- ❖ Communicates goals and self-expectations to parents and peers

❖ Develops and uses reinforcing self-statements to guard against the tendency to internalize the expectations of others

Athletes appreciate and respect the abilities they have been given and work to develop themselves to their fullest potential. Furthermore, athletes are motivated to reach their potential and will do all that is necessary to develop themselves and others to the fullest (level 7).

The athlete demonstrates disciplined, self-motivated behaviors in training and competition (levels 7 and 8) and avoids situations, people, and other lifestyle choices that are detrimental to his or her pursuit of swimming goals.

Although poor performances are disappointing, the athlete understands that poor performances and negative experiences offer an opportunity to learn from mistakes and to develop strategies for dealing with challenges that can then be applied to other difficult situations.

The athlete uses setbacks to strengthen his or her development without letting them affect the pursuit of his or her long-term goals and objectives (level 8). The athlete remains steadfast in what he or she is trying to achieve.

Drugs

Although drugs and other harmful substances are sometimes offered to or forced upon swimmers, they "Just say no" (level 1). The athlete understands the reasons why others may use performance-enhancing drugs or encourage him or her to use drugs, including the pressure to win, pressure from peers and/or teammates, and failure to make responsible decisions. Swimmers understand these temptations and still resist the pressure because they know drug use is not only wrong but also harmful (level 3).

The athlete knows the five classifications of substances banned by the International Olympic Committee (IOC), United States Olympic Committee (USOC) and the National Collegiate Athletic Association (NCAA), which include stimulants, painkillers, anabolic steroids, beta-blockers, and diuretics (level 5). Although these substances produce performance-enhancing effects, they also produce negative effects. Because the athlete is aware of these negative effects, he or she can make a wise decision regarding personal use of drugs. Following are the performance-enhancing and adverse effects of the banned substances (level 6):

❖ **Stimulants**—Purported to reduce fatigue and increase alertness, endurance, and aggressiveness. Negative side effects include insomnia, nausea, hallucinations, and depression. High doses of stimulants can lead to death.

❖ **Painkillers**—Can help the athlete push beyond a normal pain threshold. Side effects include decreased appetite, inability to concentrate, drowsiness, vomiting, fear, and dependence. Painkillers can cause severe injury by masking pain.

❖ **Anabolic steroids**—Chemical substitutes for testosterone that increase muscle bulk and strength and speed recovery from heavy training sessions. Negative side effects include increased blood pressure, increased blood fats and risk of cardiovascular disease, liver damage, hostile behavior, and growth retardation in youths.

❖ **Beta-blockers**—Cause a decrease in heart rate that is beneficial in precision sport. Drawbacks include low blood pressure, weakness, depression, numbness, and impaired endurance performance.

❖ **Diuretics**—Increase the secretion of urine, which is beneficial for athletes trying to meet a specific weight class at an event. Negative effects include stomach distress, decreased potassium, dizziness, weakness, and decreased endurance.

The swimmer understands the reason for drug testing and readily agrees to be drug tested when asked. The athlete not only resists drugs him- or herself but also takes a leadership position by encouraging others to do the same and actively participating in antidrug programs (level 8).

Time Management

Swimmers, or any athlete for that matter, devote a significant amount of time to their sport. Practice sessions and traveling to and from practice takes a great deal of time as do competitions and traveling to and from competitions. All this is in addition to an already full plate of academics, social activities, other extracurricular activities, family responsibilities, jobs, and time spent just being a kid or a teenager. It is quite a challenge for athletes to learn to balance all these demands on their time successfully.

Initially, managing time for younger athletes involves actually being on time—being on deck to swim at the start of practice, being on time for

meets (level 1). Coaches should stress the importance of punctuality and set up clear ramifications for continual tardiness. Make sure the athletes understand the importance of being on time and how timeliness demonstrates respect for coaches and teammates.

Timeliness encompasses not just physically being on time for meetings but also being timely in turning in swim-related paperwork. The athlete accepts responsibility for being on time and doing things in a time-appropriate manner (level 2).

Athletes are aware of things that make demands on their time and work to balance these demands. Prioritizing time demands helps the athlete in managing all of his or her commitments; higher priority demands take precedence in making decisions about conflicting activities.

Coaches should communicate to athletes the need to put swimming and academics high on their priority lists. Coaches should check with athletes about their academic progress and instruct them to apply the same time-management skills to school as they do in swimming, that is, being on time for class and turning in assignments when they are due (level 2).

Setting task goals and developing a weekly time schedule are effective tools for swimmers who are having difficulty balancing various time demands. It may be necessary for coaches to make accommodations during periods of intense academic demands (finals) by adjusting swimming demands. By being aware of demands on time and priorities, the swimmer is better able to balance academics with social and swimming commitments (levels 5 and 6).

Commitment and Team Loyalty

In general, athletes should develop respect and appreciation for the team, teammates, and coaches. Athletes show respect when they become aware that something is larger than themselves—an awareness that the whole is greater than the sum of the parts—and demonstrate behaviors that acknowledge this awareness.

Although swimming is primarily a co-acting sport (as opposed to an interacting sport) in that athletes compete individually, being on a team and training with teammates teach the athlete valuable skills such as effective communication, resolving conflict, and team work.

Commitment and loyalty to the team is demonstrated through an awareness of the team—team name, team colors, athletes on the team, coaches of the team, etc. (level 1). This knowledge communicates an understanding of and appreciation for something beyond themselves as individual swimmers.

Establishing team rules and traditions help foster a sense of team unity and feelings of pride in being part of the team. Making swimmers aware of the history of the team or club reinforces that the team is bigger than any one athlete or coach (level 2).

The athlete communicates pride in being part of a team by supporting his or her teammates during practices and competitions through a variety of behaviors such as speaking encouraging words, participating in team cheers, wearing team gear, and attending team gatherings (level 2).

The athlete demonstrates a respect for the sport of swimming by acquiring knowledge of the history of swimming and individual swimmers and coaches who have made an impact on the sport. The athlete is able to identify a local or national swimmer and the event in which this individual swims—a further demonstration of the athlete's awareness of the sport beyond his or her individual participation (levels 2 and 3).

Respect for the sport is reflected in an understanding of and adherence to swimming rules and standards. The athlete shows respect for the sport by seeking to excel and by doing his or her best. The athlete makes no attempts to interfere with an opponent's performance.

The athlete progresses from demonstrating commitment to the sport and the team because of external forces (rules, parents, coaches) to demonstrating commitment because of internal forces (desire, personal commitment). The athlete communicates verbally and nonverbally his or her commitment to the sport and to the team (levels 5 and 6).

The athlete understands that his or her individual commitment correlates with performance results. Furthermore, the athlete is able to look beyond personal benefits and see the positive influence he or she can have on the team and teammates by demonstrating committed behaviors (level 5).

The athlete takes a role in developing and reinforcing team goals (level 5). This may include helping to identify appropriate goals, reminding teammates of these goals on a regular basis, and monitoring behaviors that tie into the achievement of team goals. The athlete further understands and accepts team goals and sacrifices individual goals for the team (e.g., in swimming relays) in both practice and competition (level 6).

References

Clifford, C., and R. Feezell. 1997. *Coaching for Character: Reclaiming the Principles of Sportsmanship*. Champaign, IL: Human Kinetics.

Sage, G. 1998. "Does Sport Affect Character Development in Athletes?" *Journal of Physical Education, Recreation, and Dance* 69(1):15-18.

Shields, D., and B. Bredemeier. 1995. *Character Development and Physical Activity*. Champaign, IL: Human Kinetics.

Resource List

Martens, R. 1990. *Successful Coaching*. Champaign, IL: Human Kinetics.

Smith, H. 1994. *The Ten Natural Laws of Successful Time and Life Management: Proven Strategies for Increased Productivity and Inner Peace*. New York: Warner Books.

Thompson, J. 1993. *Positive Coaching: Building Character and Self-Esteem Through Sports*. Dubuque, Iowa: Brown and Benchmark.

seven

Psychology

Suzie Tuffey, PhD

The coach progressions for psychological skills parallel the athlete progressions presented in part I. Each skill is discussed in its entirety so that the coach can develop a clear understanding of the skill before trying to break it down and teach it to the athlete. As in earlier chapters, an attempt has been made to link some specific components of skill development with a level from the athlete progressions (identified in parentheses). In general, it is assumed that each skill is understood and utilized to a greater degree with increasing athlete level. Last, although much of the impetus for skill development and utilization rests with the athlete, the coach can play a big role by communicating the importance of mental skills and by integrating psychological skills training into practice.

Goal Setting

The process of goal setting can be likened to using a road map when driving a long distance. If you wanted to drive from Colorado Springs to Indianapolis (long-term goal), you would consult a map and determine the best route to use to reach your destination. You would identify the interstates and highways to take (short-term goals) and approximately how far major cities along the way are from your destination to give you feedback while driving. Similarly, athletes need to identify where they want to go (long-term goal) and how they are going to get there (short-term goals). Achieving short-term goals gives athletes feedback on how they're doing and gives them confidence in the path they have chosen.

Because athletes tend to focus exclusively on physical factors and performance outcome when setting goals, coaches should make a conscious effort to help athletes set goals that address the variety of factors that relate to athletic performance (physical, technical, psychological, nutrition, lifestyle, etc.). These goals should focus on the process of performance as opposed to solely on performance outcome.

As the coach, one of your goals should be to provide a fun environment in which the athletes are training, competing, and working towards their goals; emphasize to athletes the importance of enjoying the process of swimming and placing the process above winning. This notion of fun has been identified as a primary factor influencing continued participation in swimming (Tuffey, 1996).

Systematic goal setting provides the athlete with many benefits (level 3). An awareness of the numerous benefits of goal setting is likely to increase the chances that the athlete will set goals consistently. Goal setting accomplishes the following:

❖ **Provides direction:** Well-developed goals remind athletes where they want to go and how they are going to get there.

❖ **Enhances motivation:** Two-a-day workouts can be physically and mentally draining; reminding themselves of their goals reinforces for athletes why they are there and what they are trying to accomplish in each training session and promotes motivation and training intensity.

❖ **Builds confidence:** Reaching short-term goals can build athletes' confidence not only in their abilities but also in the path they have chosen to reach their long-term goal.

❖ **Provides feedback:** Short-term goals that are evaluated regularly provide athletes with feedback on how they are doing in progressing toward their long-term goals and help in determining if goals need to be modified.

Research lends clear support to the benefits of goal setting. Athletes need to be aware of and adhere to the following principles of goal setting, however, for it to be effective (level 4):

❖ **Set short-term and long-term goals.** Most athletes have long-term or dream goals but often fail to establish short-term goals that serve as stepping stones to long-term goals. Long-term goals alone provide no feedback or specific direction (level 5).

❖ **Set outcome and performance goals.** Most athletes set outcome goals (e.g., win the race, qualify for the state meet), but performance goals that focus on what the athletes need to *do* to perform well (e.g., maintain consistent stroke rate, streamline the body out of turns) are equally crucial. Unlike outcome goals, performance goals are in the athlete's control and allow the athlete to experience success regardless of the overall outcome.

❖ **Be specific when setting goals.** Because broad goals do not offer much guidance, focus on making goals as specific as possible (e.g., "put in a minimum of 8,000 meters in two-a-day practices six days a week" versus "train every day").

❖ **Goals are most beneficial when they are realistic and challenging.** Coaches can play a big role in helping athletes identify realistic and challenging goals. Goals that are too easy or too difficult will not provide many benefits to the athlete.

❖ **Goals, especially training goals, must be evaluated regularly.** Evaluating goals provides feedback and confidence because progress can be noted. Each athlete needs to determine what evaluated regularly means to him or her. Should goals be evaluated daily? Or should they be evaluated weekly or perhaps monthly?

Because of individual differences, athletes will probably develop different goal-setting strategies. What is important is that athletes develop and use a system that works for them; it needs to be a system to which they will adhere that also incorporates the basic principles of effective goal setting.

Through adherence to systematic goal setting, athletes can tolerate setbacks or barriers because they have a clear focus on long-term goals and confidence in their ability to reach these goals (level 7).

Imagery and Visualization

Imagery involves creating or recreating an event or a scene in one's mind. For example, an athlete can use imagery to create a perfect swim performance, or he or she can call to mind a past successful performance (level 4).

Imagery involves all the senses. When athletes are using imagery they should try to not only see but also to hear, feel, and smell all that is going on in the imagined situation. For maximal benefits, the image needs to be as close to reality as possible (level 4).

Research shows that imagery, if used purposefully, is a skill that enhances performance. But if the imagery becomes negative it can be a detriment to performance. This finding suggests that athletes need to monitor their images to keep them positive.

Make your athletes aware of the numerous ways that imagery can be used to help performance (level 4). Having this understanding will enable them to obtain the maximal benefits from imagery and will also enhance their motivation to practice and use imagery. Specifically, athletes can use imagery to do the following:

- **To see and feel success**—Athletes can use imagery to see and feel themselves achieving goals and performing as they are capable of doing. Imagery also helps enhance self-confidence.
- **To motivate**—Images of past and future competitions can be called upon to maintain persistence and intensity level while training and competing. This type of imaging provides an incentive for continued hard work.
- **To manage arousal**—Athletes can use imagery to increase or decrease arousal. For example, athletes can visualize a peaceful, relaxing scene to decrease arousal whereas motivating images can be used to increase arousal as needed.
- **To learn skills and techniques**—Athletes can use imagery as an additional form of practice to help them master a skill (e.g., athletes can visualize themselves doing a perfect flip turn prior to actual execution).
- **To refocus**—During practice and competition, many distractions and situations arise that prevent an optimal focus. Athletes can refocus themselves by using specific images to achieve the focus needed for optimal performance.
- **To prepare for competition**—Athletes can use imagery to familiarize themselves with the competitive environment and to rehearse their performance or key elements of their performance. In addition, they can use imagery to prepare for various situations that may arise so they can develop strategies to cope with these stressors. If the situation does arise they will have rehearsed it in their minds and will know how to deal with it.

Imagery is best learned and practiced in a quiet environment when the athlete is relaxed. It may be beneficial, therefore, to first discuss simple relaxation skills so that athletes learn how to relax their minds and bodies prior to learning how to use imagery (level 4).

It is helpful to develop imagery skills by initially using nonthreatening, nonstressful images (e.g., direct athletes to imagine being on a beach; encourage them to see, smell, hear, and feel the scene). The athlete can then progress to visualizing swimming skills and, finally, to imaging competitive situations.

With a little forethought, imagery training can be easily incorporated into physical training instead of making it a separate component of preparation. For example, coaches can direct athletes to visualize the technique they are working on prior to executing the drills, to imagine hard repeats to help prepare them for the challenge, or to visualize upcoming competitions to enhance practice motivation (level 6).

Athletes need to work on the following two components of imagery: *control* and *vividness*. Teach athletes to control their imagery (e.g., seeing and feeling a perfect start as opposed to visualizing the slow start that has plagued them in past races) and to make their images clear, vivid, and as close to reality as possible (e.g., they can smell the chlorine, hear their parents in the stands, and feel the muscle fatigue in the last 50 meters) (levels 7 and 8).

With continued practice athletes can manipulate images to see and feel the perfect race and see and feel themselves responding to any adverse situations. They should be able to incorporate performance cues into their visualization to create a vivid image of how they want to perform (level 8).

Self-Talk

Self-talk includes all the purposeful and random thoughts that run through the athlete's mind, the continual chatter of things said silently and out loud. Self-talk can be positive. Athletes can direct their self-talk toward what they want to do and where they want to focus. Self-talk can motivate, and, if developed purposefully, it can serve numerous other beneficial functions.

Unfortunately, self-talk can also be negative and damaging to performance (GIGO, or "garbage in, garbage out"). In fact, when left untrained, self-talk often becomes negative and critical. Therefore, the athlete must learn to manage his or her internal dialogue to keep it beneficial to performance (level 3).

As with other mental skills, the first step is awareness. Athletes need to become aware of their inner voice—what they tend to say to themselves silently and out loud and how this affects performance. Keep in mind that what may be negative and damaging to one athlete may be motivational and beneficial to another athlete (level 3).

Once aware of their self-talk and its affect on performance, athletes need to develop strategies to manage negative self-talk. One common technique used by athletes is "thought stopping," which entails the following (level 4):

- Identify negative thoughts and situations in which they typically occur.
- Practice stopping the thoughts or "parking" the thoughts.
- Replace the negative thoughts with positive thoughts, cue words, or images. Identify positive replacement thoughts in advance.

The keys to thought stopping are being aware of common negative talk; stopping the thought; and filling the void with positive, productive thoughts.

Another technique for managing negative self-talk is for athletes to identify, in advance, what they want to say to themselves or reinforce at critical points in practice and competition. Then, instead of waiting anxiously for negative thoughts to occur, the athlete automatically uses the preplanned positive self-talk. For example, an athlete who typically has defeating thoughts in the middle segment of the 1,500-meter race can develop a plan to automatically say to him- or herself, "relax, take it easy" or "stroke," during this part of the race, regardless of how he or she is feeling (levels 4 and 5).

Although it may appear that positive self-talk is most important during competition, it is equally important during practice and, therefore, must be monitored and practiced during training. Concentrating on positive self-talk in practice allows for quality training and provides an opportunity to practice this important skill.

Athletes must accept that they will experience doubts and fears. They can overcome these doubts by continually reinforcing positive, productive thoughts not just prior to competition but also on a daily basis so that positive self-talk becomes habitual. In preparation for competitions, the athlete can mentally rehearse the cue words or self-talk he or she will use throughout the race. When needed during the race, athletes can trust their training by quieting their negative self-talk and letting their bodies perform (level 8).

Arousal Control

Arousal can be best understood as having both a somatic (physical) and a cognitive (mental) component (see figure 7.1). This means that arousal has a physical effect on the athlete such as increased heart rate, increased muscle activation, increased sweating, high adrenaline, and so on. Arousal also has an effect on the athlete's cognitive functioning (self-talk, concentration, images). Although these two components are often discussed separately, it should be noted that they are inextricably linked such that change in one typically affects the other (levels 2 and 3).

An emphasis on fun and enjoyment (both in practice and competition) goes a long way towards preventing overarousal. Keeping the emphasis on fun can help alleviate the pressure the athlete feels to perform well and the expectations he or she perceives from others.

It has been found that prior to competition athletes have a specific level of arousal at which they tend to perform their best (called the *individual zone of optimal functioning (IZOF)*; see figure 7.2). The level of arousal related to best performances is highly individualized, meaning the athletes on your swim team will vary greatly in terms of their optimal arousal (levels 2-5).

Here are the steps athletes need to take to manage arousal:

1. Be aware of your optimal arousal level and the factors that increase and decrease arousal.
2. Be prepared by developing strategies to increase and decrease arousal as needed.
3. Practice using arousal management skills in a variety of situations.

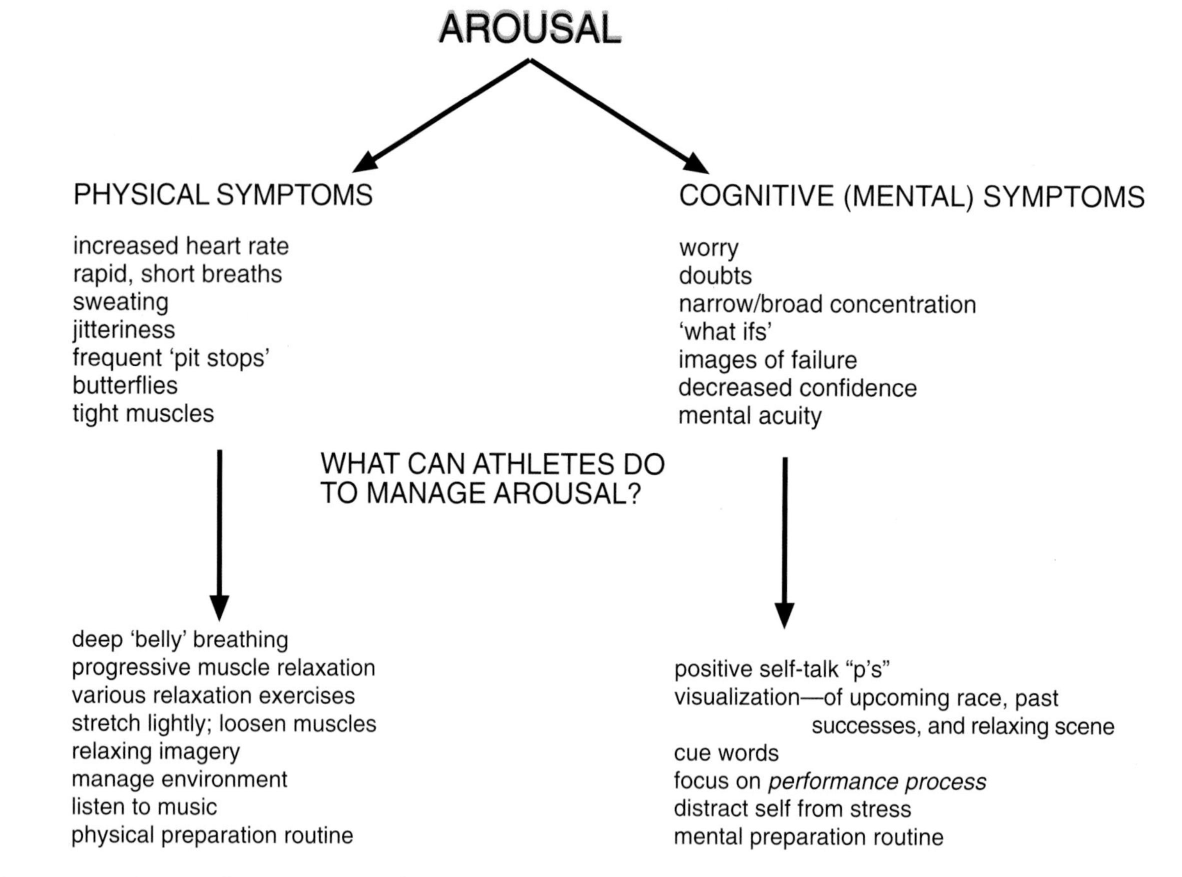

Figure 7.1 Strategies for managing arousal.

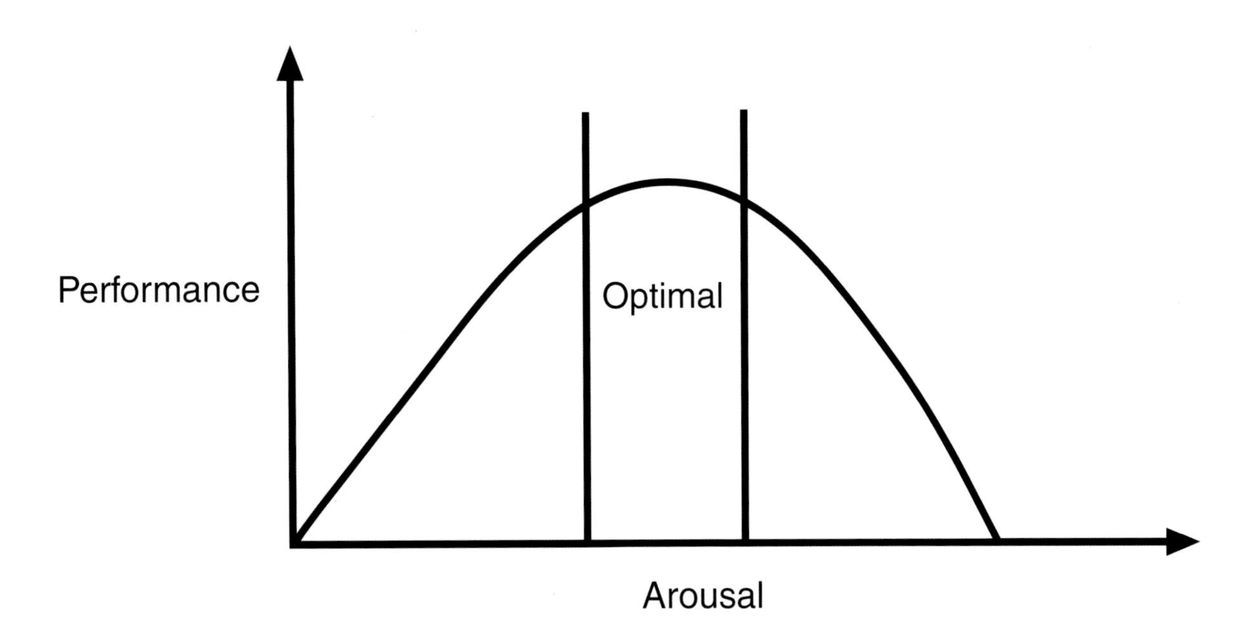

Figure 7.2 Individual zone of optimal functioning (IZOF).

Athletes need to develop an awareness of the arousal level at which they tend to perform best. They should be aware of how they need to feel physically and mentally to practice and perform well. This awareness can be achieved by evaluating past races to identify trends in how they tend to think and feel prior to good performances versus poor performances.

Athletes do not necessarily want to rid themselves of increases in physical and mental functioning. Instead, they need to know the level of arousal that is best for them and specific strategies to enable them to attain the appropriate level.

To appropriately manage arousal, it is important to differentiate between things athletes can control and things they cannot control. Athletes must learn to control and manage their reaction to a situation or event that is out of their control (an uncontrollable, or UC) (level 6). As illustrated in figure 7.1, athletes can employ a variety of strategies to manage their arousal and attain the appropriate arousal level (levels 3-6).

Athletes should prepare themselves with an arsenal of strategies to both increase and decrease their physical and mental arousal to attain a level that will be beneficial to performance. Having such an arsenal can provide athletes with a sense of control over their preparation and performance (levels 7 and 8).

Concentration

Concentration can be understood as the ability to focus attention on relevant cues and to disregard irrelevant cues. Certainly, this is not an easy task prior to competition as the athlete is typically bombarded with potentially distracting stimuli, both internally and externally (level 1).

It is helpful to conceptualize concentration along two dimensions—broad/narrow and internal/external—as illustrated in figure 7.3. The athlete needs to focus differently depending on the demands of the situation and may need to

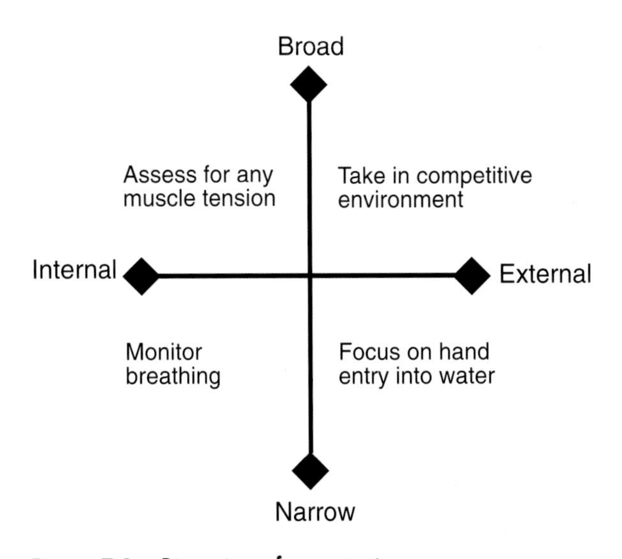

Figure 7.3 Dimensions of concentration.

shift attention from one quadrant to another quadrant as the situation changes.

Many skills are involved in effective concentration, but the primary skills involve knowing the following (levels 2-4):

1. Where to focus
2. How to focus
3. How to shift focus when necessary
4. How to refocus when distracted

Where to Focus

It is not enough for a coach to simply tell the athlete to concentrate; the athlete may have no idea what that direction means. Athletes need to understand where they should focus their attention. This focus becomes clear with a discussion of the dimensions of attention to help the athlete identify if the appropriate focus is broad or narrow, internal or external.

A review of workouts and meet performances can help identify beneficial concentration. It is helpful for athletes to think in terms of what their eyes and ears are doing. Beneficial concentration will vary among athletes. However, all athletes need to manage what they are seeing (internally and externally) and what they are hearing (internally and externally). Remind the athletes to focus on the controllables of performance (e.g., technique, stroke rate) as opposed to the uncontrollables (e.g., competitors' performance, loud fans).

How to Attain the Appropriate Focus

Once athletes are aware of where they should focus, they can use cue words, images, and focal points to bring about the desired focus. Cue words and images can be technique reminders, positive affirmations, motivating slogans, and so forth. What matters most is that the cue or image is meaningful to the athlete (e.g., putting on a cap is the cue to rehearse the upcoming performance; the image of a leopard connotes an aggressive, fast start).

How to Shift Focus

Athletes should be aware of when it is appropriate and beneficial to shift focus, and they should develop cue words, images, and focal points to help them make the shift. For example, coming out of a turn, the athlete may need to assess the field (broad–external) then return to a focus on stroke and pace (narrow–internal).

Incorporating these focusing cues into pre-race routines is extremely beneficial. Athletes should rehearse how they will focus during various segments of the race.

How to Refocus When Distracted

The first step in learning to refocus is being aware of a faulty or inappropriate focus. Next, just as when trying to focus appropriately, the athlete can use triggers, cues, focal points, etc., to reattain the desired focus. Distractions will occur so it is crucial to regard these as part of competition; swimmers need to let them go, and get back to the desired focus.

In preparation for competition it is helpful for the athlete to develop a pre-race routine to attain the appropriate focus (see Mental Preparation for Competition). Part of this preparation should be to develop and rehearse race focus points (levels 5 and 6).

With practice, the athlete should be able to manage his or her concentration (control eyes and ears) and attain a focus appropriate for the demands of the situation (level 8).

Self-Image

The nature of athletics and competition dictates that athletes will not always succeed. Failure is a part of the competitive experience. Athletes need to understand that failure offers learning experiences from which they can grow and that help them go on to achieve greater things (level 2).

Athletes not only learn through mistakes and failures but also through coach feedback. Present this feedback as a critique of the athlete's skills and not as a critique of the athlete as a person. Athletes need to accept this criticism and learn from it (level 3). Effective, sensitive communication is crucial to ensure the message is properly sent and properly received.

Athletes should become their own best friends. Instead of relying on others to boost their self-confidence and self-esteem, they must put take on that responsibility for themselves. This is accomplished, in part, by monitoring self-talk and keeping it positive and productive. Have the athletes ask themselves, "Would I allow my friends to talk to me the way I talk to myself?" (level 5).

It is important for athletes to have an understanding that the influence of self-talk extends beyond performance. Self-talk also has an impact on how athletes perceive and feel about themselves. It is crucial, therefore, for athletes to be supportive, encouraging, and positive in their daily internal dialogue and images.

As noted earlier, success and failure are a part of the competitive experience (and a part of life). With the help of others, athletes must separate performance outcome with how they feel about themselves. Whether the athlete has a good day or a bad day in training or competition should have no impact on the athlete's self-perception (level 7).

Athletes should feel they are worthy regardless of their performance. How others (coach, teammates, parents) interact with athletes after good and poor performances will have an impact on how athletes feel about themselves. Coaches and athletes should communicate this influence to all individuals involved with the athlete.

The process of striving for personal success helps instill in athletes a sense of competence and confidence in themselves as athletes and as human beings. The skills athletes develop in their athletic development will serve in other endeavors as well (level 8).

Mental Preparation for Competition

Just as athletes need to prepare themselves to compete physically, they also need to prepare themselves for competition mentally. Lack of mental preparation can have a negative impact on performance.

Swim performance can be conceptualized as a wheel, with each piece of the wheel being a factor that influences performance. The spokes of the wheel represent factors such as physical development, technique, nutrition, and the mental aspects of swimming, each of which has an influence on swim performance. Mental preparation is one piece of the wheel that needs to be purposefully addressed (level 2).

Athletes must recognize the importance of developing a precompetition routine to get their bodies and minds ready to race. A first step is for athletes to be aware of their individual zone of optimal functioning—how they need to think and feel to perform at their best (see Arousal Control). Next, athletes must develop a mental routine to help attain this optimal precompetition state. Skills such as imagery, self-talk, concentration, and arousal control (discussed in the preceding sections) help the athlete to optimally prepare his or her mind to race. A solid mental preparation routine also enables the athlete to manage potential distractions and unexpected events. With mental preparation athletes are able when necessary to "stay in their own lanes" and let their bodies do the jobs the athletes know they are capable of doing (level 7).

Resource List

Davis, M., E. Eshelman, and M. McKay. 1982. *The Relaxation and Stress Reduction Workbook*. Oakland, CA: New Harbinger.

Goldberg, A. 1997. *Sports Slump Busting*. Champaign, IL: Human Kinetics.

Martens, R. 1987. *Coaches' Guide to Sport Psychology*. Champaign, IL: Human Kinetics.

Orlick, T. 1986. *Coaches' Training Manual to Psyching for Sport*. Champaign, IL: Leisure Press.

———. 1986. *Psyching for Sport: Mental Training for Athletes*. Champaign, IL: Leisure Press.

———. 1990. *In Pursuit of Excellence: How to Win in Sport and Life Through Mental Training*. 2d ed. Champaign, IL: Leisure Press.

Tuffey, S. 1996. "Why do kids quit?" *Coaches Quarterly* 3(3): 7-8.

Vernacchia, R., R. McGuire, and D. Cook. 1996. *Coaching Mental Excellence*. Portola Valley, CA: Warde.

appendix A

Training Categories Handbook: Metabolism and Training

Jaci VanHeest, PhD

Working to Respond to the Energy Challenge

Physical work, like swimming, places energy demands on the body. The body must generate energy through pathways that break down fuel stores. These processes occur in the skeletal muscle cells and are responsive to the energy demands. Exercise training or performance can be classified in relation to both the intensity and duration of the activity. These two components are critical in generating the energy demand on the athlete.

An inverse relationship exists between exercise intensity and duration. This means that when the intensity is high the activity can only last a short period of time. On the opposite end, when duration is long the intensity that can be maintained is relatively low. One example is like the "teeter-totter" shown in figure A.1.

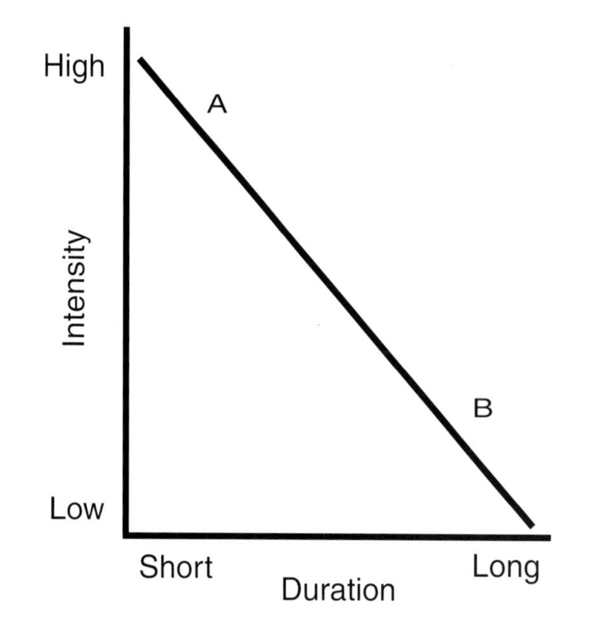

Figure A.1 Relationship between exercise intensity and duration. Point A illustrates a situation with high- intensity, short-duration work. Point B illustrates a situation with low-intensity, long-duration work.

Generation of Energy Through Metabolism

Swimming is dependent upon the constant generation of energy by the skeletal muscle. Without energy the athlete is unable to move in the water. The pathways are designed along a continuum (figure A.2). The processes always begin at the top of the line and flow down the pathways. Energy can be generated within the body in several ways, but three primary pathways are important to understand: the ATP-CP, anaerobic glycolysis, and aerobic pathways.

Adenosine triphosphate (ATP) and creatine phosphate (CP) are stored in the muscle and serve as immediate energy reservoirs. These energy stores can be utilized very rapidly but are limited in supply. This source of energy production can maintain activity for approximately 10 seconds. After this point another source of energy production must contribute for muscular contraction to continue. The ATP-CP pathway is used when energy demand is high—in short bouts of activity and at the start of exercise.

Muscle glycogen is another source for energy production in the muscle that can be maintained for longer periods of time. If the energy demand is relatively high, the muscle breaks down glycogen through anaerobic pathways. A by-product is produced during the breakdown of glycogen called *lactic acid*. The lactic acid accumulates in the muscle cells and can begin to inhibit further energy production. The glycolytic pathway can produce relatively high amounts of energy for up to about two minutes. If continued work is necessary, energy must be generated by the aerobic pathways.

When the activity lasts longer than a minute and a half to two minutes, the aerobic pathways are used. Aerobic pathways use oxygen in the process to generate energy. Energy production can be maintained for long periods of time with this system; however, the intensity of the work must be reduced.

Point to remember: The energy demand (how much and how long energy is needed) will determine the primary source of energy delivery. Intensity of exercise and duration are inversely related, meaning that highly intense work can be maintained only for short periods of time. On the other hand, low-intensity work can be performed for long periods of time.

Continuum for Metabolism

Energy for muscular movement is generated through the methods described above—aerobic and anaerobic pathways. It is important to remember that the three primary energy delivery pathways are interrelated. The contribution of each of these pathways is dependent upon the intensity and duration of the exercise.

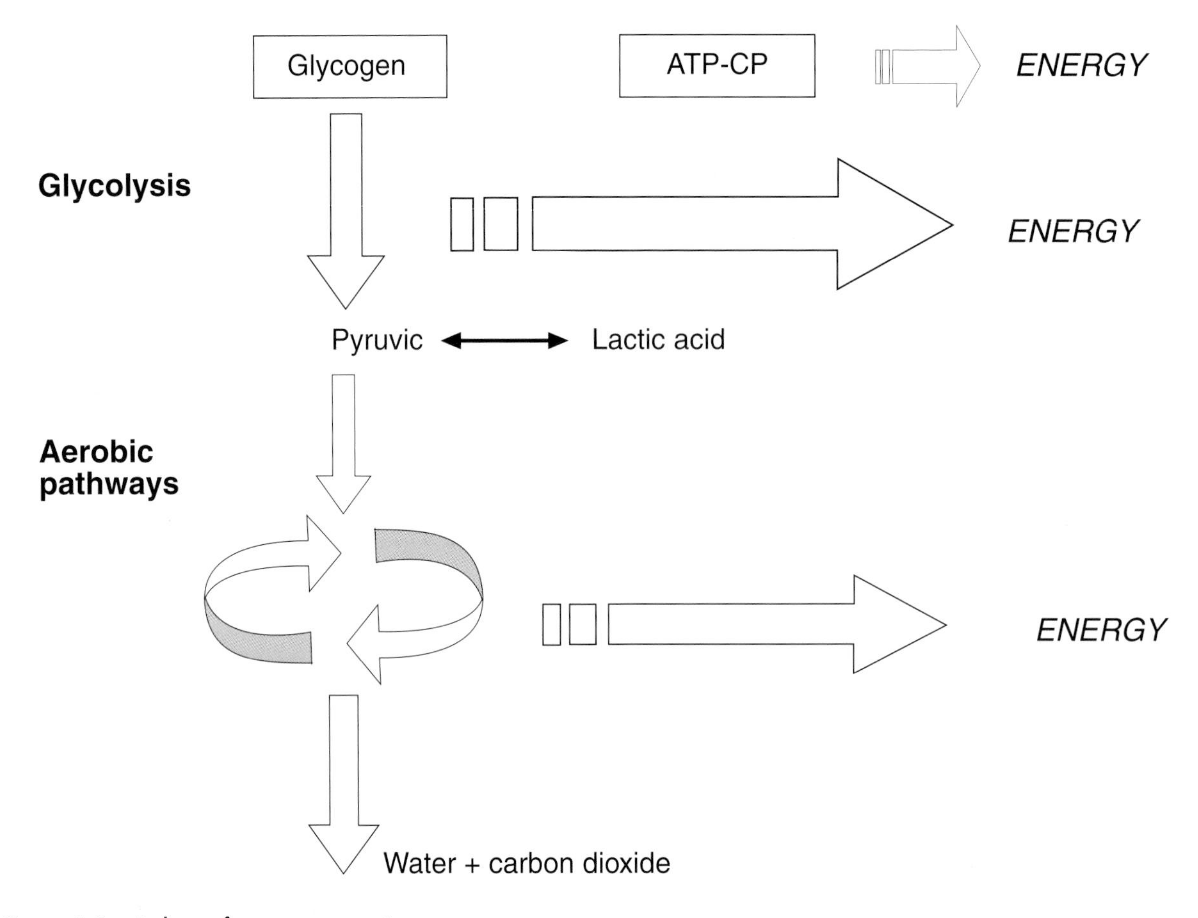

Figure A.2 Pathways for energy generation.

Training Methods

There are many ways to cause overload and adaptation in athletes. It is important that you understand the concepts of overload and individual differences. Application of these principles enables the coach to apply the appropriate training load to the swimmers.

Overload is a larger than normal training workload. This load is used to break down the swimmer's muscles to cause damage resulting in adaptation. The workload must be large enough to break down the swimmer's muscles, but not so much that the athlete cannot adapt.

Each swimmer will adapt to the training load in his or her own way and on his or her own time line. Individual differences are one reason for testing the swimmer's adaptation regularly with test sets.

Continuous Training

Straight swimming without a rest interval is considered continuous training. Continuous training is pursued in two general types—slow-paced and fast-paced. In most swimming programs, continuous training is used for warm-up or cool-down periods. The T30, or 3,000 for time swim, would be considered continuous training as well as a test set. Fast-paced continuous training (typically 80 to 90 percent of maximum heart rate) is difficult, and coaches should consider it carefully when designing athletes' training programs.

Interval Training

Interval training consists of periods of work followed by rest intervals. Interval training design comprises four primary components. Depending on the manner in which these four components are manipulated, aerobic or anaerobic pathways will be primarily taxed by the set. Here are the four components of interval training design:

- Training or swim distance
- Training interval or work time

❖ Recovery interval (rest or recovery period between swims)

❖ Repetitions of the exercise (number of swims)

Exercise intensity must be controlled to train the aerobic or anaerobic pathways. Table A.1 provides a general guide for designing interval sets for your swimmers.

USA Swimming's Training Categories

USA Swimming has developed a more specific training guide for swimmers (see table A.2). This is merely one system or strategy that can be used with your athletes to design training sets. Other viable methods exist and can be modified to fit the needs of your swimmers and your program.

Example of Interval Training Program

The chart below shows two training sets designed for a high school swimmer to improve his aerobic abilities. The coach took the athlete's best time for the 50- and 100-yard distances (35 seconds and 1 minute 20 seconds, respectively). He added 10 percent of the time to each (4 seconds and 8 seconds) to determine the training intervals of 39 seconds and 1 minute 28 seconds for each distance, respectively. These intervals caused the swimming intensity to be approximately 85 percent of the athlete's maximum heart rate. The recovery or rest interval was set at one to one (work to rest); however, this was too easy for the swimmer. Therefore, the coach reduced the interval to approximately one to one-half as shown.

Table A.1 Guidelines for Designing Interval Sets

Pathway	Intensity (% max HR)	Training interval	Recovery interval	Repetitions	Physiological adaptation
Aerobic					Increase anaerobic threshold pace
Long	80-90	2-5 min	1:1	4-6	
Short	90-95	15 sec	1:1	20-30	
Anaerobic					Improve anaerobic breakdown of glycogen and increase level of ATP-CP
Medium	95-100	60-90 sec	1:2	8-12	
Short	100	30-60 sec	1:3	15-20	

Note: Recovery interval is in proportion to exercise interval. 1:1 means work and rest are equal in time.

Set number	Training distance (yds)	Training interval (time)	Recovery interval (time)	Repetitions
One	100	1 min 28 sec	40 sec	5
Two	50	39 sec	20 sec	10

Table A.2 USA Swimming Categories for Training Athletes

Category	Purpose	Subjective intensity	Swim distance	Recovery interval	Total Set duration (actual swimming)	Expected heart rate	Intensity speed	Coach monitoring priorities	Example of a set
REC	Warm-up, cool-down, drills	Very light	Any	N/A	Any	<60% of HR max	<80% of threshold	Drills and recovery	Swim 400 easy @ HR < 120 bpm
EN1	Develop economy, maintain aerobic adaptations	Light	300-4,000	10-30 sec	15-60 minutes	60-70% of HR max	80-95% of threshold	Heart rate Stroke rate Stroke count Speed	Swim 12 x 200 with 15 sec rest @ HR = 130 bpm
EN2	Improve threshold, aerobic endurance	Somewhat hard	100-2,000	10-30 sec	15-60 minutes	70-85% of HR max	95-103% of threshold	Heart rate Stroke rate Stroke count Speed	Swim 8 x 400 with 20 sec rest @ HR = 160 bpm
EN3	Improve aerobic power and threshold (minor)	Hard	100-1,000	30-60 sec	8-30 minutes	>85% of HR max	103-107% of threshold	Stroke rate Speed Heart rate Stroke count	Swim 6 x 200 with 30-60 sec rest @ HR = 185 bpm
SP1	Improve lactate tolerance	Very hard	50-200	1:1–1:2 work to rest ratio	3-12 minutes	100% of HR max	90-95% of best 100	Speed Stroke rate Heart rate	Swim 12 x 100 on 2:30 @ holding within 3 sec of 2nd 100 split of best 200
SP2	Improve ability to produce lactate and tolerance	Extremely hard	50-100	1:2–1:8 work to rest ratio	2-6 minutes	100% of HR max	95-104% of best 100	Speed Stroke Rate	Swim 6 x 50 on 5:00 with a maximum effort on each one
SP3	Improve maximum sprint speed and power	Maximum effort sprinting	10-25	1:8+ work to rest ratio	1-2 minutes		>105% of best 100	Perfect technique and stroke rate at max. velocity for a short distance	Swim 10 x 12.5 yard or meter sprints on 2:00

appendix B

Training Categories Handbook: Ways to Obtain Aerobic Training Paces

Rick Sharp, PhD

Appendix B gives recommendations for appropriate intensities or speeds to use when designing training paces for each category. One of the ways that intensity can be prescribed for the endurance categories is based on threshold speed. The training pace charts included in this appendix for the aerobic or endurance categories (EN1, EN2, EN3) are all based on first knowing the threshold speed for the swimmer. Consequently, the coach who wishes to use the charts presented in this chapter should have a tool for estimating constant threshold speed for each swimmer.

Background on Anaerobic Threshold

In 1976 Mader, Heck, and Hollman described a method whereby endurance training speeds could be prescribed based on the individual's blood lactate response to different swimming paces. Mader inferred that speeds corresponding to a blood lactate of four millimolar (4 mM) would provide the best stimulus for improving endurance capacity because faster speeds could not be maintained long enough to provide the appropriate aerobic stimulus, and slower speeds would typically underload the endurance systems.

Because measurements of blood lactate were out of reach for most coaches, a considerable amount of work was done to identify simpler, safer, and less expensive ways of prescribing a threshold speed.

T30 or Timed 3,000 Swim

The T30, or 3,000 swim for time, gives the coach a pretty good idea of each athlete's ability to sustain prolonged work. This works if the swimmer puts forth an honest effort; the maximum speed the swimmer can maintain is his or her individual continuous swimming threshold speed.

In 1985 Olbrecht, Madsen, Mader, Liesen, and Hollmann reported the results of a study that was designed to test the validity of various training sets in predicting a swimmer's 4 mM threshold speed. The volunteers for the study were 59 members of the German Men's National team. They were first tested for their 4 mM speed using Mader's two-speed test and were then asked to swim various interval sets, a 30-minute swim as fast as possible, and a 60-minute swim as fast as possible. The major finding of the study was that swimmers chose a pace during their 30-minute swim that was not significantly different from their 4 mM speed. From this finding the authors concluded that the 30-minute swim test could be used to estimate a swimmer's 4 mM threshold speed without the need of blood sampling. Since then, the 30-minute swim test has been referred to as the T30.

To perform this test a swimmer can either do the T30 test exactly as Olbrecht et al. described, swim continuously for 25 to 40 minutes, or swim a timed 3,000 and calculate the average pace per 100 meters or yards.

Instructions for T30

1. Measure the distance the swimmer covers in a 30-minute continuous swim. It must be an honest effort by the swimmer to cover as much distance as possible using an even pace.
2. Calculate the average pace per 100 meters or yards.

   Example: Swimmer goes 2,650 yards during his or her T30 swim

$$\frac{30\text{ minutes}}{2650\text{ yards}} \times \frac{100\text{ yards}}{1\text{ repeat}} =$$

$$\frac{1.132\text{ minutes}}{1\text{ repeat}} \times \frac{60\text{ seconds}}{1\text{ minute}} =$$

$$\frac{67.9\text{ seconds}}{1\text{ repeat}} \text{ or } \frac{1:07.9\text{ minutes}}{1\text{ repeat}}$$

3. Alternatively, you can use the pacing chart in table B.1 on page 98 to find the 100 pace corresponding to the distance swum in the T30.

Instructions for Timed 3,000

1. Have the swimmer swim a 3,000 for time (or other distance that will equal approximately 30 minutes) with honest effort and even pace.
2. Calculate the average pace per 100.
3. Alternatively, you can use the pacing charts in tables B.2 or B.3 (pp. 99-101) to find the 100 pace corresponding to the distance swum for the 3,000 for time.

Training Pace Charts Based on T30

Why are three times given for each training pace prescription?

The standard deviation for the prediction of threshold from a T30 test has been shown to be plus or minus 0.053 meters/second. Therefore, prescribed paces should fall within a range of plus or minus 0.053 meters/second, acknowledging that 68 percent of the population will have a threshold within this range (based on the research). Because swimming speed is more easily prescribed as time for given distances, the 0.053 meters/second standard deviation has been converted to actual times. Thus, each distance has a fast speed (prescribed pace plus 0.053 meters/second), the prescribed pace, and a slower speed (prescribed pace minus 0.053 meters/second) for the swimmer to stay within. The coach should remember that although a range of paces is given based on the research, this range only covers about 68 percent of the swimmers. Therefore, some swimmers will be able to swim faster than this prescribed range, and some will have to swim slower than the paces given here (see tables B.5 and B.6 on pages 103 and 104). In using these paces, it makes sense to start a set at the slower end of the prescribed range and gradually descend to the faster end of the range. If the swimmer does not seem to be able to hold a pace within the prescribed range for the length of an EN2 set, the coach might conclude that this swimmer is one of those who fall outside of the 68 percent who are covered by the standard deviation. In this case, the swimmer should be allowed to swim somewhat slower than the prescribed range so that EN2 sets can be performed with a constant speed without undue fatigue.

Why are paces for distances shorter than 400 so much faster than the threshold pace?

If the goal is to stay close to a blood lactate level corresponding to that occurring during a long threshold swim (e.g., T30), the previously identified threshold pace must be adjusted for short-duration swims. The shorter the repeats, the faster the pace needs to be to generate an equivalent lactate accumulation as would occur in long swims. In addition, when 30 seconds of rest is used instead of 10 seconds, the adjustments need to be even greater. For example, a swimmer swam a T30 and averaged one minute five seconds per 100 yards. Based on the EN2 10-second rest chart, he or she would need to average about one minute three seconds during an EN2 set of 24 × 100 yards. Averaging a time of one minute five seconds on this set would be physiologically easier than it would be during continuous swimming. Research has also shown that such adjustment is not necessary when repeats are over 400 meters. Thus, in tables B.5 through B.6 (pp. 103-104) adjustments are made at the shorter distances.

How were the EN1 paces derived?

In theory, any speed slower than threshold speed but still fast enough to create some aerobic adaptations could be used for an EN1 speed. For convenience, the EN1 speeds shown in the EN1 chart in table B.4 on page 102 are simply five percent slower than the EN2-10 seconds speed (with the faster and slower speed based on the standard deviation also included).

How were the EN3 speeds determined?

Again, swimming any speed that is faster than threshold will probably target the correct adaptations one looks for in doing EN3 training *as long as the set is constructed properly*. However, to give coaches an approximate idea of what these speeds usually are, the EN3 speeds shown in table B.7 on page 105 were set at a range three percent, five percent, and seven percent faster than the average speed prescribed in table B.6 on page 104.

References

Mader, A., Heck, H., and Hollman, W. 1976. "Evaluation of lactic acid anaerobic energy contribution by determination of post-exercise lactic acid concentration of capillary blood in middle distance runners and swimmers." In F. Landing and W. Orban (Eds.), *Exercise Physiology*, 187-199.

Olbrecht, J., O. Madsen, A. Mader, H. Liesen, and W. Hollmann. 1985. "Relationship Between Swimming Velocity and Lactic Acid Concentration During Continuous and Intermittent Training Exercises." *International Journal of Sports Medicine* 6(2):74-77.

	Repeats	50	75	100	150	200	300	400
EN2-10 sec	% speed increase	9%	6%	3%	2.25%	1.5%	0.75%	0%
EN2-30 sec	% speed increase	14.5%	10.9%	7.3%	4.9%	2.5%	1.5%	0.5%

Table B.1 Number of Lengths Completed in a 30-Minute Swim

Total yards or meters	# lengths swum, yards	# lengths swum, meters	Average pace per 100	Total yards or meters	# lengths swum, yards	# lengths swum, meters	Average pace per 100
3500	140	70	:51.4	2300	92	46	1:18.3
3475	139	69.5	:51.8	2275	91	45.5	1:19.1
3450	138	69	:52.2	2250	90	45	1:20.0
3425	137	68.5	:52.6	2225	89	44.5	1:20.9
3400	136	68	:52.9	2200	88	44	1:21.8
3375	135	67.5	:53.3	2175	87	43.5	1:22.8
3350	134	67	:53.7	2150	86	43	1:23.7
3325	133	66.5	:54.1	2125	85	42.5	1:24.7
3300	132	66	:54.5	2100	84	42	1:25.7
3275	131	65.5	:55.0	2075	83	41.5	1:26.7
3250	130	65	:55.4	2050	82	41	1:27.8
3225	129	64.5	:55.8	2025	81	40.5	1:28.9
3200	128	64	:56.3	2000	80	40	1:30.0
3175	127	63.5	:56.7	1975	79	39.5	1:31.1
3150	126	63	:57.1	1950	78	39	1:32.3
3125	125	62.5	:57.6	1925	77	38.5	1:33.5
3100	124	62	:58.1	1900	76	38	1:34.7
3075	123	61.5	:58.5	1875	75	37.5	1:36.0
3050	122	61	:59.0	1850	74	37	1:37.3
3025	121	60.5	:59.5	1825	73	36.5	1:38.6
3000	120	60	1:00.0	1800	72	36	1:40.0
2975	119	59.5	1:00.5	1775	71	35.5	1:41.4
2950	118	59	1:01.0	1750	70	35	1:42.9
2925	117	58.5	1:01.5	1725	69	34.5	1:44.3
2900	116	58	1:02.1	1700	68	34	1:45.9
2875	115	57.5	1:02.6	1675	67	33.5	1:47.5
2850	114	57	1:03.2	1650	66	33	1:49.1
2825	113	56.5	1:03.7	1625	65	32.5	1:50.8
2800	112	56	1:04.3	1600	64	32	1:52.5
2775	111	55.5	1:04.9	1575	63	31.5	1:54.3
2750	110	55	1:05.5	1550	62	31	1:56.1
2725	109	54.5	1:06.1	1525	61	30.5	1:58.0
2700	108	54	1:06.7	1500	60	30	2:00.0
2675	107	53.5	1:07.3	1475	59	29.5	2:02.0
2650	106	53	1:07.9	1450	58	29	2:04.1
2625	105	52.5	1:08.6	1425	57	28.5	2:06.3
2600	104	52	1:09.2	1400	56	28	2:08.6
2575	103	51.5	1:09.9	1375	55	27.5	2:10.9
2550	102	51	1:10.6	1350	54	27	2:13.3
2525	101	50.5	1:11.3	1325	53	26.5	2:15.8
2500	100	50	1:12.0	1300	52	26	2:18.5
2475	99	49.5	1:12.7	1275	51	25.5	2:21.2
2450	98	49	1:13.5	1250	50	25	2:24.0
2425	97	48.5	1:14.2	1225	49	24.5	2:26.9
2400	96	48	1:15.0	1200	48	24	2:30.0
2375	95	47.5	1:15.8	1175	47	23.5	2:33.2
2350	94	47	1:16.6	1150	46	23	2:36.5
2325	93	46.5	1:17.4	1125	45	22.5	2:40.0

Used to calculate EN2 or "threshold pPace"

Table B.2 Time Trials

100	800	1000	1500	1650	2000	3000
0:48.0	06:24	08:00	12:00	13:12	16:00	24:00
0:48.5	06:28	08:05	12:07	13:20	16:10	24:15
0:49.0	06:32	08:10	12:15	13:28	16:20	24:30
0:49:5	06:36	08:15	12:23	13:37	16:30	24:45
0:50.0	06:40	08:20	12:30	13:45	16:40	25:00
0:50.5	06:44	08:25	12:37	13:53	16:50	25:15
0:51.0	06:48	08:30	12:45	14:01	17:00	25:30
0:51.5	06:52	08:35	12:52	14:10	17:10	25:45
0:52.0	06:56	08:40	13:00	14:18	17:20	26:00
0:52.5	07:00	08:45	13:08	14:26	17:30	26:15
0:53.0	07:04	08:50	13:15	14:35	17:40	26:30
0:53.5	07:08	08:55	13:22	14:43	17:50	26:45
0:54.0	07:12	09:00	13:30	14:51	18:00	27:00
0:54.5	07:16	09:05	13:37	14:59	18:10	27:15
0:55.0	07:20	09:10	13:45	15:07	18:20	27:30
0:55.5	07:24	09:15	13:52	15:16	18:30	27:45
0:56.0	07:28	09:20	14:00	15:24	18:40	28:00
0:56.5	07:32	09:25	14:08	15:32	18:50	28:15
0:57.0	07:36	09:30	14:15	15:40	19:00	28:30
0:57.5	07:40	09:35	14:22	15:49	19:10	28:45
0:58.0	07:44	09:40	14:30	15:57	19:20	29:00
0:58.5	07:48	09:45	14:37	16:05	19:30	29:15
0:59.0	07:52	09:50	14:45	16:14	19:40	29:30
0:59.5	07:56	09:55	14:52	16:22	19:50	2945
1:00.0	08:00	10:00	15:00	16:30	20:00	30:00
1:00.5	08:04	10:05	15:07	16:38	20:10	30:15
1:01.0	08:08	10:10	15:15	16:46	20:20	30:30
1:01.5	08:12	10:15	15:22	16:55	20:30	30:45
1:02.0	08:16	10:20	15:30	17:03	20:40	31:00
1:02.5	08:20	10:25	15:38	17:11	20:50	31:15
1:03.0	08:24	10:30	15:45	17:19	21:00	21:30
1:03.5	08:28	10:35	15:53	17:28	21:10	31:45
1:04.0	08:32	10:40	16:00	17:36	21:20	32:00
1:04.5	08:36	10:45	16:07	17:44	21:30	32:15
1:05.0	08:40	10:50	16:15	17:52	21:40	32:30
1:05.5	08:44	10:55	16:22	18:01	21:50	32:45
1:06.0	08:48	11:00	16:30	18:09	22:00	33:00
1:06.5	08:52	11:05	16:38	18:17	22:10	33:15
1:07.0	08:56	11:10	16:45	18:26	22:20	33:30
1:07.5	09:00	11:15	16:52	18:34	22:30	33:45
1:08.0	09:04	11:20	17:00	18:42	22:40	34:00
1:08.5	09:08	11:25	17:07	18:50	22:50	34:15
1:09.0	09:12	11:30	17:15	18:58	23:00	34:30
1:09.5	09:16	11:35	17:22	19:07	23:10	34:45
1:10.0	09:20	11:40	17:30	19:15	23:20	35:00
1:10.5	09:24	11:45	17:38	19:23	23:30	35:15
1:11.0	09:28	11:50	17:45	19:31	23:40	35:30
1:11.5	09:32	11:55	17:52	19:40	23:50	35:45
1:12.0	09:36	12:00	18:00	19:48	24:00	36:00
1:12.5	09:40	12:05	18:07	19:56	24:10	36:15
1:13.0	09:44	12:10	18:15	20:05	24:20	36:30
1:13.5	09:48	12:15	18:23	20:13	24:30	36:45

100	800	1000	1500	1650	2000	3000
1:14.0	09:52	12:20	18:30	20:21	24:40	37:00
1:14.5	09:56	12:25	18:38	20:29	24:50	37:15
1:15.0	10:00	12:30	18:45	20:37	25:00	37:30
1:15.5	10:04	12:35	18:52	20:46	25:10	37:45
1:16.0	10:08	12:40	19:00	20:54	25:20	38:00
1:16.5	10:12	12:45	19:07	21:02	25:30	38:15
1:17.0	10:16	12:50	19:15	21:10	25:40	38:30
1:17.5	10:20	12:55	19:22	21:19	25:50	38:45
1:18.0	10:24	13:00	19:30	21:27	26:00	39:00
1:18.5	10:28	13:05	19:37	21:35	26:10	39:15
1:19.0	10:32	13:10	19:45	21:44	26:20	39:30
1:19.5	10:36	13:15	19:52	21:52	26:30	39:45
1:20.0	10:40	13:20	20:00	22:00	26:40	40:00
1:20.5	10:44	13:25	20:08	22:08	26:50	40:15
1:21.0	10:48	13:30	20:15	22:16	27:00	40:30
1:21.5	10:52	13:35	20:22	22:25	27:10	40:45
1:22.0	10:56	13:40	20:30	22:33	27:20	41:00
1:22.5	11:00	13:45	20:37	22:41	27:30	41:15
1:23.0	11:04	13:50	20:45	22:49	27:40	41:30
1:23.5	11:08	13:55	20:52	22:58	27:50	41:45
1:24.0	11:12	14:00	21:00	23:06	28:00	42:00
1:24.5	11:16	14:05	21:07	23:14	28:10	42:15
1:25.0	11:20	14:10	21:15	23:23	28:20	42:30
1:25.5	11:24	14:15	21:23	23:31	28:30	42:45
1:26.0	11:28	14:20	21:30	23:39	28:40	43:00
1:26.5	11:32	14:25	21:37	23:47	28:50	43:15
1:27.0	11:36	14:30	21:45	23:55	29:00	43:30
1:27.5	11:40	14:35	21:52	24:04	29:10	43:45
1:28.0	11:44	14:40	22:00	24:12	29:20	44:00
1:28.5	11:48	14:45	22:08	24:20	29:30	44:15
1:29.0	11:52	14:50	22:15	24:28	29:40	44:30
1:29.5	11:56	14:55	22:23	24:37	29:50	44:45
1:30.0	12:00	15:00	22:30	24:45	30:00	45:00
1:30.5	12:04	15:05	22:37	24:53	30:10	45:15
1:31.0	12:08	15:10	22:45	25:01	30:20	45:30
1:31.5	12:12	15:15	22:52	25:10	30:30	45:45
1:32.0	12:16	15:20	23:00	25:18	30:40	46:00
1:32.5	12:20	15:25	23:08	25:26	30:50	46:15
1:33.0	12:24	15:30	23:15	25:35	31:00	46:30
1:33.5	12:28	15:35	23:22	25:43	31:10	46:45
1:34.0	12:32	15:40	23:30	25:51	31:20	47:00
1:34.5	12:36	15:45	23:37	25:59	31:30	47:15
1:35.0	12:40	15:50	23:45	26:08	31:40	47:30
1:35.5	12:44	15:55	23:52	26:16	31:50	47:45
1:36.0	12:48	16:00	24:00	26:24	32:00	48:00
1:36.5	12:52	16:05	24:08	26:32	32:10	48:15
1:37.0	12:56	16:10	24:15	26:40	32:20	48:30
1:37.5	13:00	16:15	24:22	26:49	32:30	48:45
1:38.0	13:04	16:20	24:30	26:57	32:40	49:00
1:38.5	13:08	16:25	24:37	27:05	32:50	49:15
1:39.0	13:12	16:30	24:45	27:14	33:00	49:30
1:39.5	13:16	16:35	24:52	27:22	33:10	49:45

100	800	1000	1500	1650	2000	3000
1:40.0	13:20	16:40	25:00	27:30	33:20	50:00
1:40.5	13:24	16:45	25:07	27:38	33:30	50:15
1:41.0	13:28	16:50	25:15	27:46	33:40	50:30
1:41.5	13:32	16:55	25:22	27:55	33:50	50:45
1:42.0	13:36	17:00	25:30	28:03	34:00	51:00
1:42.5	13:40	17:05	25:38	28:11	34:10	51:15
1:43.0	13:44	17:10	25:45	28:19	34:20	51:30
1:43.5	13:48	17:15	25:53	28:28	34:30	51:45
1:44.0	13:52	17:20	26:00	28:36	34:40	52:00
1:44.5	13:56	17:25	26:08	28:44	34:50	52:15
1:45.0	14:00	17:30	26:15	28:53	35:00	52:30
1:45.5	14:04	17:35	26:22	29:01	35:10	52:45
1:46.0	14:08	17:40	26:30	29:09	35:20	53:00
1:46.5	14:12	17:45	26:37	29:17	35:30	53:15
1:47.0	14:16	17:50	26:45	29:25	35:40	53:30
1:47.5	14:20	17:55	26:52	29:34	35:50	53:45
1:48.0	14:24	18:00	27:00	29:42	36:00	54:00
1:48.5	14:28	18:05	27:07	29:50	36:10	54:15
1:49.0	14:32	18:10	27:15	29:58	36:20	54:30
1:49.5	14:36	18:15	27:22	30:07	36:30	54:45
1:50.0	14:40	18:20	27:30	30:15	36:40	55:00
1:50.5	14:44	18:25	27:38	30:23	36:50	55:15
1:51.0	14:48	18:30	27:45	30:32	37:00	55:30
1:51.5	14:52	18:35	27:53	30:40	37:10	55:45
1:52.0	14:56	18:40	28:00	30:48	37:20	56:00
1:52.5	15:00	18:45	28:07	30:56	37:30	56:15
1:53.0	15:04	18:50	28:15	31:05	37:40	56:30
1:53.5	15:08	18:55	28:22	31:13	37:50	56:45
1:54.0	15:12	19:00	28:30	31:21	38:00	57:00
1:54.5	15:16	19:05	28:37	31:29	38:10	57:15
1:55.0	15:20	19:10	28:45	31:37	38:20	57:30
1:55.5	15:24	19:15	28:52	31:46	38:30	57:45
1:56.0	15:28	19:20	29:00	31:54	38:40	58:00
1:56.5	15:32	19:25	29:07	32:02	38:50	58:15
1:57.0	15:36	19:30	29:15	32:11	39:00	58:30
1:57.5	15:40	19:35	29:22	32:19	39:10	58:45
1:58.0	15:44	19:40	29:30	32:27	39:20	59:00
1:58.5	15:48	19:45	29:38	32:35	39:30	59:15
1:59.0	15:52	19:50	29:45	32:44	39:40	59:30
1:59.5	15:56	19:55	29:52	32:52	39:50	59:45
2:00.0	16:00	20:00	30:00	33:00	44:00	60:00

"100" column is the average pace per 100 used to calculate EN2 or "threshold pace."

Table B.3 Pacing Chart for Determining Training Paces During a Distance Swim

100	200	300	400	500	600	700	800	900	1000	1100	1200	1300	1400	1500	1600	1650
0:48	01:36	02:24	03:12	04:00	04:48	05:36	06:24	07:12	08:00	08:48	09:36	10:24	11:12	12:00	12:48	13:12
0:49	01:38	02:27	03:16	04:05	04:54	05:43	06:32	07:21	08:10	08:59	09:48	10:37	11:26	12:15	13:04	13:28.5
0:50	01:40	02:30	03:20	04:10	05:00	05:50	06:40	07:30	08:20	09:10	10:00	10:50	11:40	12:30	13:20	13:45
0:51	01:42	02:33	03:24	04:15	05:06	05:57	06:48	07:39	08:30	09:21	10:12	11:03	11:54	12:45	13:36	14:01.5
0:52	01:44	02:36	03:28	04:20	05:12	06:04	06:56	07:48	08:40	09:32	10:24	11:16	12:08	13:00	13:52	14:18
0:53	01:46	02:39	03:32	04:25	05:18	06:11	07:04	07:57	08:50	09:43	10:36	11:29	12:22	13:15	14:08	14:34.5
0:54	01:48	02:42	03:36	04:30	05:24	06:18	07:12	08:06	09:00	09:54	10:48	11:42	12:36	13:30	14:24	14:51
0:55	01:50	02:45	03:40	04:35	05:30	06:25	07:20	08:15	09:10	10:05	11:00	11:55	12:50	13:45	14:40	15:07.5
0:56	01:52	02:48	03:44	04:40	05:36	06:32	07:28	08:24	09:20	10:16	11:12	12:08	13:04	14:00	14:56	15:24
0:57	01:54	02:51	03:48	04:45	05:42	06:39	07:36	08:33	09:30	10:27	11:24	12:21	13:18	14:15	15:12	15:40.5
0:58	01:56	02:54	03:52	04:50	05:48	06:46	07:44	08:42	09:40	10:38	11:36	12:34	13:32	14:30	15:28	15:57
0:59	01:58	02:57	03:56	04:55	05:54	06:53	07:52	08:51	09:50	10:49	11:48	12:47	13:46	14:45	15:44	16:13.5
1:00	02:00	03:00	04:00	05:00	06:00	07:00	08:00	09:00	10:00	11:00	12:00	13:00	14:00	15:00	16:00	16:30
1:01	02:02	03:03	04:04	05:05	06:06	07:07	08:08	09:09	10:10	11:11	12:12	13:13	14:14	15:15	16:16	16:46.5
1:02	02:04	03:06	04:08	05:10	06:12	07:14	08:16	09:18	10:20	11:22	12:24	13:26	14:28	15:30	16:32	17:03
1:03	02:06	03:09	04:12	05:15	06:18	07:21	08:24	09:27	10:30	11:33	12:36	13:39	14:42	15:45	16:48	17:19.5
1:04	02:08	03:12	04:16	05:20	06:24	07:28	08:32	09:36	10:40	11:44	12:48	13:52	14:56	16:00	17:04	17:36
1:05	02:10	03:15	04:20	05:25	06:30	07:35	08:40	09:45	10:50	11:55	13:00	14:05	15:10	16:15	17:20	17:52.5
1:06	02:12	03:18	04:24	05:30	06:36	07:42	08:48	09:54	11:00	12:06	13:12	14:18	15:24	16:30	17:36	18:09
1:07	02:14	03:21	04:28	05:35	06:42	07:49	08:56	10:03	11:10	12:17	13:24	14:31	15:38	16:45	17:52	18:25.5
1:08	02:16	03:24	04:32	05:40	06:48	07:56	09:04	10:12	11:20	12:28	13:36	14:44	15:52	17:00	18:08	18:42
1:09	02:18	03:27	04:36	05:45	06:54	08:03	09:12	10:21	11:30	12:39	13:48	14:57	16:06	17:15	18:24	18:58.5
1:10	02:20	03:30	04:40	05:50	07:00	08:10	09:20	10:30	11:40	12:50	14:00	15:10	16:20	17:30	18:40	19:15
1:11	02:22	03:33	04:44	05:55	07:06	08:17	19:28	10:39	11:50	13:01	14:12	15:23	16:34	17:45	18:56	19:31.5
1:12	02:24	03:36	04:48	06:00	07:12	08:24	09:36	10:48	12:00	13:12	14:24	15:36	16:48	18:00	19:12	19:48
1:13	02:26	03:39	04:52	06:05	07:18	08:31	09:44	10:57	12:10	13:23	14:36	15:49	17:02	18:15	19:28	20:04.5
1:14	02:28	03:42	04:56	06:10	07:24	08:38	09:52	11:06	12:20	13:34	14:48	16:02	17:16	18:30	19:44	20:21
1:15	02:30	03:45	05:00	06:15	07:30	08:45	10:00	11:15	12:30	13:45	15:00	16:15	17:30	18:45	20:00	20:37.5
1:16	02:32	03:48	05:04	06:20	07:36	08:52	10:08	11:24	12:40	13:56	15:12	16:28	17:44	19:00	20:16	20:54
1:17	02:34	03:51	05:08	06:25	07:42	08:59	10:16	11:33	12:50	14:07	15:24	16:41	17:58	19:15	20:32	21:10.5
1:18	02:36	03:54	05:12	06:30	07:48	09:06	10:24	11:42	13:00	14:18	15:36	16:54	18:12	19:30	20:48	21:27
1:19	02:38	03:57	05:16	06:35	07:54	09:13	10:32	11:51	13:10	14:29	15:48	17:07	18:26	19:45	21:04	21:43.5
1:20	02:40	04:00	05:20	06:40	08:00	09:20	10:40	12:00	13:20	14:40	16:00	17:20	18:40	20:00	21:20	22:00
1:21	02:42	04:03	05:24	06:45	08:06	09:27	10:48	12:09	13:30	14:51	16:12	17:33	18:54	20:15	21:36	22:16.5
1:22	02:44	04:06	05:28	06:50	08:12	09:34	10:56	12:18	13:40	15:02	16:24	17:46	19:08	20:30	21:52	22:33
1:23	02:46	04:09	05:32	06:55	08:18	09:41	11:04	12:27	13:50	15:13	16:36	17:59	19:22	20:45	22:08	22:49.5
1:24	02:48	04:12	05:36	07:00	08:24	09:48	11:12	12:36	14:00	15:24	16:48	18:12	19:36	21:00	22:24	23:06
1:25	02:50	04:15	05:40	07:05	08:30	09:55	11:20	12:45	14:10	15:35	17:00	18:25	19:50	21:15	22:40	23:22.5
1:26	02:52	04:18	05:44	07:10	08:36	10:02	11:28	12:54	14:20	15:46	17:12	18:38	20:04	21:30	22:56	23:39
1:27	02:54	04:21	05:48	07:15	08:42	10:09	11:36	13:03	14:30	15:57	17:24	18:51	20:18	21:45	23:12	23:55.5
1:28	02:56	04:24	05:52	07:20	08:48	10:16	11:44	13:12	14:40	16:08	17:36	19:04	20:32	22:00	23:28	24:12
1:29	02:58	04:27	05:56	07:25	08:54	10:23	11:52	13:21	14:50	16:19	17:48	19:17	20:46	22:15	23:44	24:28.5
1:30	03:00	04:30	06:00	07:30	09:00	10:30	12:00	13:30	15:00	16:30	18:00	19:30	21:00	22:30	24:00	24:45
1:31	03:02	04:33	06:04	07:35	09:06	10:37	12:08	13:39	15:10	16:41	18:12	19:43	21:14	22:45	24:16	25:01.5
1:32	03:04	04:36	06:08	07:40	09:12	10:44	12:16	13:48	15:20	16:52	18:24	19:56	21:28	23:00	24:32	25:18
1:33	03:06	04:39	06:12	07:45	09:18	10:51	12:24	13:57	15:30	17:03	18:36	20:09	21:42	23:15	24:48	25:34.5
1:34	03:08	04:42	06:16	07:50	09:24	10:58	12:32	14:06	15:40	17:14	18:48	20:22	21:56	23:30	25:04	25:51
1:35	03:10	04:45	06:20	07:55	09:30	11:05	12:40	14:15	15:50	17:25	19:00	20:35	22:10	23:45	25:20	26:07.5
1:36	03:12	04:48	06:24	08:00	09:36	11:12	12:48	14:24	16:00	17:36	19:12	20:48	22:24	24:00	25:36	26:24
1:37	03:14	04:51	06:28	08:05	09:42	11:19	12:56	14:33	16:10	17:47	19:24	21:01	22:38	24:15	25:52	26:40.5
1:38	03:16	04:54	06:32	08:10	09:48	11:26	13:04	14:42	16:20	17:58	19:36	21:14	22:52	24:30	26:08	26:57
1:39	03:18	04:57	06:36	08:15	09:54	11:33	13:12	14:51	16:30	18:09	19:48	21:27	23:06	24:45	26:24	27:13.5
1:40	03:20	05:00	06:40	08:20	10:00	11:40	13:20	15:00	16:40	18:20	20:00	21:40	23:20	25:00	26:40	27:30

100	1700	1800	1900	2000	2100	2200	2300	2400	2500	2600	2700	2800	2900	3000	3100	3200
0:48	13:36	14:24	15:12	16:00	16:48	17:36	18:24	19:12	20:00	20:48	21:36	22:24	23:12	24:00	24:48	25:36
0:49	13:53	14:42	15:31	16:20	17:09	17:58	18:47	19:36	20:25	21:14	22:03	22:52	23:41	24:30	25:19	26:08
0:50	14:10	15:00	15:50	16:40	17:30	18:20	19:10	20:00	20:50	21:40	22:30	23:20	24:10	25:00	25:50	26:40
0:51	14:27	15:18	16:09	17:00	17:51	18:42	19:33	20:24	21:15	22:06	22:57	23:48	24:39	25:30	26:21	27:12
0:52	14:44	15:36	16:28	17:20	18:12	19:04	19:56	20:48	21:40	22:32	23:24	24:16	25:08	26:00	26:52	27:44
0:53	15:01	15:54	16:47	17:40	18:33	19:26	20:19	21:12	22:05	22:58	23:51	24:44	25:37	26:30	27:23	28:16
0:54	15:18	16:12	17:06	18:00	18:54	19:48	20:42	21:36	22:30	23:24	24:18	25:12	26:06	27:00	27:54	28:48
0:55	15:35	16:30	17:25	18:20	19:15	20:10	21:05	22:00	22:55	23:50	24:45	25:40	26:35	27:30	28:25	29:20
0:56	15:52	16:48	17:44	18:40	19:36	20:32	21:28	22:24	23:20	24:16	25:12	26:08	27:04	28:00	28:56	29:52
0:57	16:09	17:06	18:03	19:00	19:57	20:54	21:51	22:48	23:45	24:42	25:39	26:36	27:33	28:30	29:27	30:24
0:58	16:26	17:24	18:22	19:20	20:18	21:16	22:14	23:12	24:10	25:08	26:06	27:04	28:02	29:00	29:58	30:56
0:59	16:43	17:42	18:42	19:40	20:39	21:38	22:37	23:36	24:35	25:34	26:33	27:32	28:31	29:30	30:29	31:28
1:00	17:00	18:00	19:00	20:00	21:00	22:00	23:00	24:00	25:00	26:00	27:00	28:00	29:00	30:00	31:00	32:00
1:01	17:17	18:18	19:19	20:20	21:21	22:22	23:23	24:24	25:25	26:26	27:27	28:28	29:29	30:30	31:31	32:32
1:02	17:34	18:36	19:38	20:40	21:42	22:44	23:46	24:48	25:50	26:52	27:54	28:56	29:58	31:00	32:02	33:04
1:03	17:51	18:54	19:57	21:00	22:03	23:06	24:09	25:12	26:15	27:18	28:21	29:24	30:27	31:30	32:33	33:36
1:04	18:08	19:12	20:16	21:20	22:24	23:28	24:32	25:36	26:40	27:44	28:48	29:52	30:56	32:00	33:04	34:08
1:05	18:25	19:30	20:35	21:40	22:45	23:50	24:55	26:00	27:05	28:10	29:15	30:20	31:25	32:30	33:35	34:40
1:06	18:42	19:48	20:54	22:00	23:06	24:12	25:18	26:24	27:30	28:36	29:42	30:48	31:54	33:00	34:06	35:12
1:07	18:59	20:06	21:13	22:20	23:27	24:34	25:41	26:48	27:55	29:02	30:09	31:16	32:23	33:30	34:37	35:44
1:08	19:16	20:24	21:32	22:40	23:48	24:56	26:04	27:12	28:20	29:28	30:36	31:44	32:52	34:00	35:08	36:16
1:09	19:33	20:42	21:51	23:00	24:09	25:18	26:27	27:36	28:45	29:54	31:03	32:12	33:21	34:30	35:39	36:48
1:10	19:50	21:00	22:10	23:20	24:30	25:40	26:50	28:00	29:10	30:20	31:30	32:40	33:50	35:00	36:10	37:20
1:11	20:07	21:18	22:29	23:40	24:51	26:02	27:13	28:24	29:35	30:46	31:57	33:08	34:19	35:30	36:41	37:52
1:12	20:24	21:36	22:48	24:00	25:12	26:24	27:36	28:48	30:00	31:12	32:24	33:36	34:48	36:00	37:12	38:24
1:13	20:41	21:54	23:07	24:20	25:33	26:46	27:59	29:12	30:25	31:38	32:51	34:04	35:17	36:30	37:43	38:56
1:14	20:58	22:12	23:26	24:40	25:54	27:08	28:22	29:36	30:50	32:04	33:18	34:32	35:46	37:00	38:14	39:28
1:15	21:15	22:30	23:45	25:00	26:15	27:30	28:45	30:00	31:15	32:30	33:45	35:00	36:15	37:30	38:45	40:00
1:16	21:32	22:48	24:04	25:20	26:36	27:52	29:08	30:24	31:40	32:56	34:12	35:28	36:44	38:00	39:16	40:32
1:17	21:49	23:06	24:23	25:40	26:57	28:14	29:31	30:48	32:05	33:22	34:39	35:56	37:13	38:30	39:47	41:04
1:18	22:06	23:24	24:42	26:00	27:18	28:36	29:54	31:12	32:30	33:48	35:06	36:24	37:42	39:00	40:18	41:36
1:19	22:23	23:42	25:01	26:20	27:39	28:58	30:17	31:36	32:55	34:14	35:33	36:52	38:11	39:30	40:49	42:08
1:20	22:40	24:00	25:20	26:40	38:00	29:20	30:40	32:00	33:20	34:40	36:00	37:20	38:40	40:00	41:20	42:40
1:21	22:57	24:18	25:39	27:00	28:21	29:42	31:03	32:24	33:45	35:06	36:27	37:48	39:09	40:30	41:51	43:12
1:22	23:14	24:36	25:58	27:20	28:42	30:04	31:26	32:48	34:10	35:32	36:54	38:16	39:38	41:00	42:22	43:44
1:23	23:31	24:54	26:17	27:40	29:03	30:26	31:49	33:12	34:35	35:58	37:21	38:44	40:07	41:30	42:53	44:16
1:24	23:48	25:12	26:36	28:00	29:24	30:48	32:12	33:36	35:00	36:24	37:48	39:12	40:36	42:00	43:24	44:48
1:25	24:05	25:30	26:55	28:20	29:45	31:10	32:35	34:00	35:25	36:50	38:15	39:40	41:05	42:30	43:55	45:20
1:26	24:22	25:48	27:14	28:40	30:06	31:32	32:58	34:24	35:50	37:16	38:42	40:08	41:34	43:00	44:26	45:52
1:27	24:39	26:06	27:33	29:00	30:27	31:54	33:21	34:48	36:15	37:42	39:09	40:36	42:03	43:30	44:57	46:24
1:28	24:56	26:24	27:52	29:20	30:48	32:16	33:44	35:12	36:40	38:08	39:36	41:04	42:32	44:00	45:28	46:56
1:29	25:13	26:42	28:11	29:40	31:09	32:38	34:07	35:36	37:05	38:34	40:03	41:32	43:01	44:30	45:59	47:28
1:30	25:30	27:00	28:30	30:00	31:30	33:00	34:30	36:00	37:30	39:00	40:30	42:00	43:30	45:00	46:30	48:00
1:31	25:47	27:18	28:49	30:20	31:51	33:22	34:53	36:24	37:55	39:26	40:57	42:28	43:59	45:30	47:01	48:32
1:32	26:04	27:36	29:08	30:40	32:12	33:44	35:16	36:48	38:20	39:52	41:24	42:56	44:28	46:00	47:32	49:04
1:33	26:21	27:54	29:27	31:00	32:33	34:06	35:39	37:12	38:45	40:18	41:51	43:24	44:57	46:30	48:03	49:36
1:34	26:38	28:12	29:46	31:20	32:54	34:28	36:02	37:36	39:10	40:44	42:18	43:52	45:26	47:00	48:34	50:08
1:35	26:55	28:30	30:05	31:40	33:15	34:50	36:25	38:00	39:35	41:10	42:45	44:20	45:55	47:30	49:05	50:40
1:36	27:12	28:48	30:24	32:00	33:36	35:12	36:48	38:24	40:00	41:36	43:12	44:48	46:24	48:00	49:36	51:12
1:37	27:29	29:06	30:43	32:20	33:57	35:34	37:11	38:48	40:25	42:02	43:39	45:16	46:53	48:30	50:07	51:44
1:38	27:46	29:24	31:02	32:40	34:18	35:56	67:34	39:12	40:50	42:28	44:06	45:44	47:22	49:00	50:38	52:16
1:39	28:03	29:42	31:21	33:00	34:39	36:18	37:57	39:36	41:15	42:54	44:33	46:12	47:51	49:30	51:09	52:48
1:40	28:20	30:00	31:40	33:20	35:00	36:40	38:20	10:00	41:40	43:20	45:00	46:40	48:20	50:00	51:40	53:20

Table B.4 EN1-10 Seconds Rest

Repeat distance

Threshold	25	50	75	100	150	200	300	400	500
0:55	0:13	0:26	0:40	0:54	1:22	1:51	2:47	3:44	4:41
	0:13	**0:26**	**0:41**	**0:56**	**1:25**	**1:54**	**2:52**	**3:51**	**4:49**
	0:13	0:27	0:42	0:58	1:27	1:57	2:57	3:58	4:57
0:56	0:13	0:26	0:40	0:55	1:24	1:53	2:50	3:48	4:46
	0:13	**0:27**	**0:42**	**0:57**	**1:26**	**1:56**	**2:55**	**3:55**	**4:54**
	0:14	0:28	0:43	0:59	1:29	1:59	3:00	4:02	5:03
0:57	0:13	0:27	0:41	0:56	1:25	1:54	2:53	3:52	4:50
	0:13	**0:27**	**0:42**	**0:58**	**1:28**	**1:58**	**2:58**	**3:59**	**4:59**
	0:14	0:28	0:44	1:00	1:31	2:02	3:04	4:07	5:09
0:58	0:13	0:27	0:42	0:57	1:27	1:56	2:56	3:56	4:55
	0:14	**0:28**	**0:43**	**0:59**	**1:29**	**2:00**	**3:01**	**4:04**	**5:05**
	0:14	0:29	0:44	1:01	1:32	2:04	3:07	4:11	5:14
0:59	0:13	0:28	0:43	0:58	1:28	1:58	2:59	4:00	5:00
	0:14	**0:28**	**0:44**	**1:00**	**1:31**	**2:02**	**3:04**	**4:08**	**5:10**
	0:14	0:29	0:45	1:02	1:34	2:06	3:10	4:16	5:20
1:00	0:14	0:28	0:43	0:59	1:30	2:00	3:02	4:04	5:05
	0:14	**0:29**	**0:45**	**1:01**	**1:32**	**2:04**	**3:08**	**4:12**	**5:15**
	0:15	0:30	0:46	1:03	1:35	2:08	3:14	4:20	5:25
1:01	0:14	0:28	0:44	1:00	1:31	2:02	3:05	4:08	5:10
	0:14	**0:29**	**0:45**	**1:02**	**1:34**	**2:06**	**3:11**	**4:16**	**5:20**
	0:15	0:30	0:47	1:04	1:37	2:10	3:17	4:25	5:31
1:02	0:14	0:29	0:45	1:01	1:32	2:04	3:08	4:12	5:15
	0:15	**0:30**	**0:46**	**1:03**	**1:36**	**2:08**	**3:14**	**4:20**	**5:26**
	0:15	0:31	0:48	1:05	1:39	2:13	3:20	4:29	5:37
1:03	0:14	0:29	0:45	1:02	1:34	2:06	3:11	4:16	5:20
	0:15	**0:30**	**0:47**	**1:04**	**1:37**	**2:10**	**3:17**	**4:25**	**5:31**
	0:15	0:31	0:48	1:06	1:40	2:15	3:24	4:34	5:42
1:04	0:15	0:30	0:46	1:03	1:35	2:08	3:14	4:20	5:25
	0:15	**0:31**	**0:48**	**1:05**	**1:39**	**2:12**	**3:20**	**4:29**	**5:36**
	0:16	0:32	0:49	1:08	1:42	2:17	3:27	4:38	5:48
1:05	0:15	0:30	0:47	1:04	1:37	2:10	3:16	4:24	5:30
	0:15	**0:31**	**0:48**	**1:06**	**1:40**	**2:14**	**3:23**	**4:33**	**5:41**
	0:16	0:32	0:50	1:09	1:44	2:19	3:30	4:43	5:53
1:06	0:15	0:31	0:47	1:05	1:38	2:12	3:19	4:28	5:35
	0:15	**0:32**	**0:49**	**1:07**	**1:42**	**2:17**	**3:26**	**4:37**	**5:47**
	0:16	0:33	0:51	1:10	1:45	2:22	3:34	4:47	5:59
1:07	0:15	0:31	0:48	1:06	1:40	2:14	3:22	4:32	5:40
	0:16	**0:32**	**0:50**	**1:08**	**1:43**	**2:19**	**3:29**	**4:41**	**5:52**
	0:16	0:33	0:52	1:11	1:47	2:24	3:37	4:52	6:05
1:08	0:15	0:32	0:49	1:07	1:41	2:16	3:25	4:36	5:45
	0:16	**0:33**	**0:51**	**1:09**	**1:45**	**2:21**	**3:33**	**4:46**	**5:57**
	0:17	0:34	0:52	1:12	1:49	2:26	3:41	4:56	6:10
1:09	0:16	0:32	0:49	1:08	1:43	2:18	3:28	4:40	5:49
	0:16	**0:33**	**0:51**	**1:10**	**1:46**	**2:23**	**3:36**	**4:50**	**6:02**
	0:17	0:34	0:53	1:13	1:50	2:28	3:44	5:01	6:16
1:10	0:16	0:33	0:50	1:09	1:44	2:20	3:31	4:43	5:54
	0:16	**0:34**	**0:52**	**1:11**	**1:48**	**2:25**	**3:39**	**4:54**	**6:08**
	0:17	0:35	0:54	1:14	1:52	2:30	3:47	5:05	6:22
1:11	0:16	0:33	0:51	1:10	1:45	2:22	3:34	4:47	5:59
	0:17	**0:34**	**0:53**	**1:12**	**1:49**	**2:27**	**3:42**	**4:58**	**6:13**
	0:17	0:36	0:55	1:15	1:54	2:33	3:51	5:10	6:27
1:12	0:16	0:33	0:52	1:11	1:47	2:23	3:37	4:51	6:04
	0:17	**0:35**	**0:53**	**1:13**	**1:51**	**2:29**	3:45	5:02	6:18
	0:18	0:36	0:56	1:16	1:55	2:35	3:54	5:14	6:33
1:13	0:16	0:34	0:52	1:12	1:48	2:25	3:40	4:55	6:09
	0:17	**0:35**	**0:54**	**1:14**	**1:52**	**2:31**	**3:48**	**5:07**	**6:23**
	0:18	0:37	0:56	1:17	1:57	2:37	3:57	5:19	6:39
1:14	0:17	0:34	0:53	1:13	1:50	2:27	3:43	4:59	6:14
	0:17	**0:36**	**0:55**	**1:15**	**1:54**	**2:33**	**3:51**	**5:11**	**6:29**
	0:18	0:37	0:57	1:19	1:59	2:39	4:01	5:23	6:44
1:15	0:17	0:35	0:54	1:14	1:51	2:29	3:46	5:03	6:19
	0:18	**0:36**	**0:56**	**1:16**	**1:56**	**2:35**	**3:54**	**5:15**	**6:34**
	0:18	0:38	0:58	1:20	2:00	2:42	4:04	5:28	6:50
1:16	0:17	0:35	0:54	1:14	1:53	2:31	3:48	5:07	6:24
	0:18	**0:37**	**0:56**	**1:17**	**1:57**	**2:37**	**3:58**	**5:19**	**6:39**
	0:19	0:38	0:59	1:21	2:02	2:44	4:08	5:33	6:56
1:17	0:17	0:36	0:55	1:15	1:54	2:33	3:51	5:11	6:28
	0:18	**0:37**	**0:57**	**1:18**	**1:59**	**2:39**	**4:01**	**5:23**	**6:44**
	0:19	0:39	1:00	1:22	2:04	2:46	4:11	5:37	7:01
1:18	0:18	0:36	0:56	1:16	1:55	2:35	3:54	5:15	6:33
	0:18	**0:38**	**0:58**	**1:20**	**2:00**	**2:41**	**4:04**	**5:28**	**6:50**
	0:19	0:39	1:00	1:23	2:05	2:48	4:14	5:42	7:07
1:19	0:18	0:37	0:56	1:17	1:57	2:37	3:57	5:18	6:38
	0:19	**0:38**	**0:59**	**1:21**	**2:02**	**2:43**	**4:07**	**5:32**	**6:55**
	0:19	0:40	1:01	1:24	2:07	2:51	4:18	5:46	7:13
1:20	0:18	0:37	0:57	1:18	1:58	2:39	4:00	5:22	6:43
	0:19	**0:39**	**0:59**	**1:22**	**2:03**	**2:46**	**4:10**	**5:36**	**7:00**
	0:20	0:40	1:02	1:25	2:09	2:53	4:21	5:51	7:19

Repeat distance

Threshold	25	50	75	100	150	200	300	400	500
1:21	0:18	0:37	0:58	1:19	2:00	2:41	4:03	5:26	6:48
	0:19	**0:39**	**1:00**	**1:23**	**2:05**	**2:48**	**4:13**	**5:40**	**7:05**
	0:20	0:41	1:03	1:26	2:10	2:55	4:25	5:55	7:24
1:22	0:18	0:38	0:58	1:20	2:01	2:43	4:06	5:30	6:53
	0:19	**0:39**	**1:01**	**1:24**	**2:06**	**2:50**	**4:16**	**5:44**	**7:11**
	0:20	0:41	1:04	1:27	2:12	2:57	4:28	6:00	7:30
1:23	0:19	0:38	0:59	1:21	2:02	2:44	4:09	5:34	6:57
	0:19	**0:40**	**1:02**	**1:25**	**2:08**	**2:52**	**4:20**	**5:49**	**7:16**
	0:20	0:42	1:05	1:29	2:14	3:00	4:31	6:05	7:36
1:24	0:19	0:39	1:00	1:22	2:04	2:46	4:11	5:38	7:02
	0:20	**0:40**	**1:02**	**1:26**	**2:09**	**2:54**	**4:23**	**5:53**	**7:21**
	0:21	0:42	1:05	1:30	2:15	3:02	4:35	6:09	7:42
1:25	0:19	0:39	1:00	1:23	2:05	2:48	4:14	5:42	7:07
	0:20	**0:41**	**1:03**	**1:27**	**2:11**	**2:56**	**4:26**	**5:57**	**7:26**
	0:21	0:43	1:06	1:31	2:17	3:04	4:38	6:14	7:47
1:26	0:19	0:40	1:01	1:24	2:07	2:50	4:17	5:45	7:12
	0:20	**0:41**	**1:04**	**1:28**	**2:12**	**2:58**	**4:29**	**6:01**	**7:32**
	0:21	0:43	1:07	1:32	2:19	3:06	4:42	6:18	7:53
1:27	0:19	0:40	1:02	1:25	2:08	2:52	4:20	5:49	7:17
	0:20	**0:42**	**1:05**	**1:29**	**2:14**	**3:00**	**4:32**	**6:05**	**7:37**
	0:21	0:44	1:08	1:33	2:20	3:09	4:45	6:23	7:59
1:28	0:20	0:40	1:02	1:26	2:10	2:54	4:23	5:53	7:21
	0:21	**0:42**	**1:05**	**1:30**	**2:16**	**3:02**	**4:35**	**6:10**	**7:42**
	0:22	0:44	1:09	1:34	2:22	3:11	4:49	6:28	8:05
1:29	0:20	0:41	1:03	1:27	2:11	2:56	4:26	5:57	7:26
	0:21	**0:43**	**1:06**	**1:31**	**2:17**	**3:04**	**4:38**	**6:14**	**7:47**
	0:22	0:45	1:09	1:35	2:24	3:13	4:52	6:32	8:10
1:30	0:20	0:41	1:04	1:28	2:12	2:58	4:29	6:01	7:31
	0:21	**0:43**	**1:07**	**1:32**	**2:19**	**3:06**	**4:41**	**6:18**	**7:53**
	0:22	0:46	1:10	1:36	2:26	3:16	4:55	6:37	8:16
1:31	0:20	0:42	1:04	1:28	2:14	3:00	4:31	6:05	7:36
	0:21	**0:44**	**1:08**	**1:33**	**2:20**	**3:08**	**4:45**	**6:22**	**7:58**
	0:22	0:46	1:11	1:37	2:27	3:18	4:59	6:42	8:22
1:32	0:21	0:42	1:05	1:29	2:15	3:01	4:34	6:08	7:41
	0:22	**0:44**	**1:08**	**1:34**	**2:22**	**3:10**	**4:48**	**6:26**	**8:03**
	0:23	0:47	1:12	1:39	2:29	3:20	5:02	6:46	8:28
1:33	0:21	0:43	1:06	1:30	2:17	3:03	4:37	6:12	7:45
	0:22	**0:45**	**1:09**	**1:35**	**2:23**	**3:12**	**4:51**	**6:31**	**8:08**
	0:23	0:47	1:13	1:40	2:31	3:22	5:06	6:51	8:34
1:34	0:21	0:43	1:07	1:31	2:18	3:05	4:40	6:16	7:50
	0:22	**0:45**	**1:10**	**1:36**	**2:25**	**3:14**	**4:54**	**6:35**	**8:14**
	0:23	0:48	1:13	1:41	2:32	3:25	5:09	6:56	8:39
1:35	0:21	0:44	1:07	1:32	2:19	3:07	4:43	6:20	7:55
	0:22	**0:46**	**1:11**	**1:37**	**2:26**	**3:17**	**4:57**	**6:39**	**8:19**
	0:23	0:48	1:14	1:42	2:34	3:27	5:13	7:00	8:45
1:36	0:21	0:44	1:08	1:33	2:21	3:09	4:46	6:24	8:00
	0:23	**0:46**	**1:11**	**1:38**	**2:28**	**3:19**	**5:00**	**6:43**	**8:24**
	0:24	0:49	1:15	1:43	2:36	3:29	5:16	7:05	8:51
1:37	0:22	0:44	1:09	1:34	2:22	3:11	4:48	6:27	8:04
	0:23	**0:47**	**1:12**	**1:39**	**2:29**	**3:21**	**5:03**	**6:47**	**8:29**
	0:24	0:49	1:16	1:44	2:38	3:32	5:20	7:09	8:57
1:38	0:22	0:45	1:09	1:35	2:24	3:13	4:51	6:31	8:09
	0:23	**0:47**	**1:13**	**1:40**	**2:31**	**3:23**	**5:06**	**6:52**	**8:35**
	0:24	0:50	1:17	1:45	2:39	3:34	5:23	7:14	9:03
1:39	0:22	0:45	1:10	1:36	2:25	3:15	4:54	6:35	8:14
	0:23	**0:48**	**1:14**	**1:41**	**2:32**	**3:25**	**5:10**	**6:56**	**8:40**
	0:24	0:50	1:18	1:47	2:41	3:36	5:27	7:19	9:09
1:40	0:22	0:46	1:11	1:37	2:26	3:16	4:57	6:39	8:19
	0:23	**0:48**	**1:14**	**1:42**	**2:34**	**3:27**	**5:13**	**7:00**	**8:45**
	0:25	0:51	1:18	1:48	2:43	3:38	5:30	7:24	9:14
1:41	0:22	0:46	1:11	1:38	2:28	3:18	5:00	6:43	8:23
	0:24	**0:49**	**1:15**	**1:43**	**2:36**	**3:29**	**5:16**	**7:04**	**8:50**
	0:25	0:51	1:19	1:49	2:44	3:41	5:34	7:28	9:20
1:42	0:23	0:47	1:12	1:39	2:29	3:20	5:03	6:46	8:28
	0:24	**0:49**	**1:16**	**1:44**	**2:37**	**3:31**	**5:19**	**7:08**	**8:56**
	0:25	0:52	1:20	1:50	2:46	3:43	5:37	7:33	9:26
1:43	0:23	0:47	1:13	1:40	2:30	3:22	5:05	6:50	8:33
	0:24	**0:50**	**1:17**	**1:45**	**2:39**	**3:33**	**5:22**	**7:13**	**9:01**
	0:26	0:52	1:21	1:51	2:48	3:45	5:41	7:38	9:32
1:44	0:23	0:47	1:13	1:40	2:32	3:24	5:08	6:54	8:37
	0:24	**0:50**	**1:17**	**1:46**	**2:40**	**3:35**	**5:25**	**7:17**	**9:06**
	0:26	0:53	1:22	1:52	2:50	3:48	5:44	7:42	9:38
1:45	0:23	0:48	1:14	1:41	2:33	3:26	5:11	6:58	8:42
	0:25	**0:51**	**1:18**	**1:47**	**2:42**	**3:37**	**5:28**	**7:21**	**9:11**
	0:26	0:54	1:23	1:53	2:51	3:50	5:48	7:47	9:44
1:46	0:24	0:48	1:15	1:42	2:35	3:28	5:14	7:02	8:47
	0:25	**0:51**	**1:19**	**1:48**	**2:43**	**3:39**	**5:31**	**7:25**	**9:17**
	0:26	0:54	1:23	1:54	2:53	3:52	5:51	7:52	9:50

Table B.5 EN2-10 Seconds Rest

Repeat distance

Threshold	50	75	100	150	200	300	400	500
0:55	0:25	0:38	0:52	1:18	1:45	2:39	3:34	4:27
	0:25	**0:39**	**0:53**	**1:21**	**1:48**	**2:44**	**3:40**	**4:35**
	0:26	0:40	0:55	1:23	1:52	2:49	3:47	4:43
0:56	0:25	0:38	0:53	1:20	1:47	2:42	3:38	4:32
	0:26	**0:40**	**0:54**	**1:22**	**1:50**	**2:47**	**3:44**	**4:40**
	0:26	0:41	0:56	1:25	1:54	2:52	3:51	4:49
0:57	0:25	0:39	0:54	1:21	1:49	2:45	3:41	4:37
	0:26	**0:40**	**0:55**	**1:24**	**1:52**	**2:50**	**3:48**	**4:45**
	0:27	0:42	0:57	1:26	1:56	2:55	3:55	4:54
0:58	0:26	0:40	0:55	1:23	1:51	2:48	3:45	4:41
	0:27	**0:41**	**0:56**	**1:25**	**1:54**	**2:53**	**3:52**	**4:50**
	0:27	0:42	0:58	1:28	1:58	2:58	3:59	4:59
0:59	0:26	0:40	0:56	1:24	1:53	2:50	3:49	4:46
	0:27	**0:42**	**0:57**	**1:27**	**1:56**	**2:56**	**3:56**	**4:55**
	0:28	0:43	0:59	1:29	2:00	3:01	4:04	5:05
1:00	0:27	0:41	0:56	1:25	1:55	2:53	3:53	4:51
	0:28	**0:42**	**0:58**	**1:28**	**1:58**	**2:59**	**4:00**	**5:00**
	0:28	0:44	1:00	1:31	2:02	3:05	4:08	5:10
1:01	0:27	0:42	0:57	1:27	1:56	2:56	3:56	4:55
	0:28	**0:43**	**0:59**	**1:29**	**2:00**	**3:02**	**4:04**	**5:05**
	0:29	0:45	1:01	1:32	2:04	3:08	4:12	5:15
1:02	0:28	0:42	0:58	1:28	1:58	2:59	4:00	5:00
	0:28	**0:44**	**1:00**	**1:31**	**2:02**	**3:05**	**4:08**	**5:10**
	0:29	0:45	1:02	1:34	2:06	3:11	4:16	5:21
1:03	0:28	0:43	0:59	1:29	2:00	3:02	4:04	5:05
	0:29	**0:45**	**1:01**	**1:32**	**2:04**	**3:08**	**4:12**	**5:15**
	0:30	0:46	1:03	1:36	2:08	3:14	4:21	5:26
1:04	0:28	0:44	1:00	1:31	2:02	3:04	4:08	5:10
	0:29	**0:45**	**1:02**	**1:34**	**2:06**	**3:11**	**4:16**	**5:20**
	0:30	0:47	1:04	1:37	2:11	3:17	4:25	5:31
1:05	0:29	0:44	1:01	1:32	2:04	3:07	4:11	5:14
	0:30	**0:46**	**1:03**	**1:35**	**2:08**	**3:14**	**4:20**	**5:25**
	0:31	0:48	1:05	1:39	2:13	3:20	4:29	5:37
1:06	0:29	0:45	1:02	1:34	2:06	3:10	4:15	5:19
	0:30	**0:47**	**1:04**	**1:37**	**2:10**	**3:17**	**4:24**	**5:30**
	0:31	0:48	1:06	1:40	2:15	3:24	4:34	5:42
1:07	0:30	0:46	1:03	1:35	2:07	3:13	4:19	5:24
	0:31	**0:47**	**1:05**	**1:38**	**2:12**	**3:20**	**4:28**	**5:35**
	0:32	0:49	1:07	1:42	2:17	3:27	4:38	5:47
1:08	0:30	0:46	1:04	1:36	2:09	3:15	4:23	5:28
	0:31	**0:48**	**1:06**	**1:40**	**2:14**	**3:22**	**4:32**	**5:40**
	0:32	0:50	1:08	1:43	2:19	3:30	4:42	5:53
1:09	0:31	0:47	1:05	1:38	2:11	3:18	4:26	5:33
	0:32	**0:49**	**1:07**	**1:41**	**2:16**	**3:25**	**4:36**	**5:45**
	0:33	0:51	1:10	1:45	2:21	3:33	4:46	5:58
1:10	0:31	0:48	1:06	1:39	2:13	3:21	4:30	5:37
	0:32	**0:50**	**1:08**	**1:43**	**2:18**	**3:28**	**4:40**	**5:50**
	0:33	0:51	1:11	1:47	2:23	3:36	4:51	6:03
1:11	0:31	0:48	1:06	1:40	2:15	3:24	4:34	5:42
	0:33	**0:50**	**1:09**	**1:44**	**2:20**	**3:31**	**4:44**	**5:55**
	0:34	0:52	1:12	1:48	2:25	3:40	4:55	6:09
1:12	0:32	0:49	1:07	1:42	2:17	3:27	4:37	5:47
	0:33	**0:51**	**1:10**	**1:46**	**2:22**	**3:34**	**4:48**	**6:00**
	0:34	0:53	1:13	1:50	2:28	3:43	4:59	6:14
1:13	0:32	0:50	1:08	1:43	2:18	3:29	4:41	5:51
	0:33	**0:52**	**1:11**	**1:47**	**2:24**	**3:37**	**4:52**	**6:05**
	0:35	0:54	1:14	1:51	2:30	3:46	5:04	6:20
1:14	0:33	0:50	1:09	1:44	2:20	3:32	4:45	5:56
	0:34	**0:52**	**1:12**	**1:49**	**2:26**	**3:40**	**4:56**	**6:10**
	0:35	0:54	1:15	1:53	2:32	3:49	5:08	6:25
1:15	0:33	0:51	1:10	1:46	2:22	3:35	4:49	6:01
	0:34	**0:53**	**1:13**	**1:50**	**2:28**	**3:43**	**5:00**	**6:15**
	0:36	0:55	1:16	1:55	2:34	3:53	5:12	6:31
1:16	0:34	0:52	1:11	1:47	2:24	3:38	4:52	6:05
	0:35	**0:54**	**1:14**	**1:51**	**2:30**	**3:46**	**5:04**	**6:20**
	0:36	0:56	1:17	1:56	2:36	3:56	5:17	6:36
1:17	0:34	0:52	1:12	1:49	2:26	3:40	4:56	6:10
	0:35	**0:54**	**1:15**	**1:53**	**2:32**	**3:49**	**5:08**	**6:25**
	0:37	0:57	1:18	1:58	2:38	3:59	5:21	6:41
1:18	0:34	0:53	1:13	1:50	2:28	3:43	5:00	6:15
	0:36	**0:55**	**1:16**	**1:54**	**2:34**	**3:52**	**5:12**	**6:30**
	0:37	0:58	1:19	1:59	2:40	4:02	5:25	6:47
1:19	0:35	0:54	1:14	1:51	2:29	3:46	5:03	6:19
	0:36	**0:56**	**1:17**	**1:56**	**2:36**	**3:55**	**5:16**	**6:35**
	0:38	0:58	1:20	2:01	2:42	4:06	5:30	6:52
1:20	0:35	0:54	1:15	1:53	2:31	3:49	5:07	6:24
	0:37	**0:57**	**1:18**	**1:57**	**2:38**	**3:58**	**5:20**	**6:40**
	0:38	0:59	1:21	2:03	2:45	4:09	5:34	6:58

Repeat distance

Threshold	50	75	100	150	200	300	400	500
1:21	0:36	0:55	1:15	1:54	2:33	3:51	5:11	6:28
	0:37	**0:57**	**1:19**	**1:59**	**2:40**	**4:01**	**5:24**	**6:45**
	0:39	1:00	1:22	2:04	2:47	4:12	5:39	7:03
1:22	0:36	0:56	1:16	1:55	2:35	3:54	5:14	6:33
	0:38	**0:58**	**1:20**	**2:00**	**2:42**	**4:04**	**5:28**	**6:50**
	0:39	1:01	1:23	2:06	2:49	4:15	5:43	7:09
1:23	0:36	0:56	1:17	1:57	2:37	3:57	5:18	6:38
	0:38	**0:59**	**1:21**	**2:02**	**2:44**	**4:07**	**5:32**	**6:55**
	0:40	1:01	1:24	2:07	2:51	4:19	5:47	7:14
1:24	0:37	0:57	1:18	1:58	2:38	3:59	5:22	6:42
	0:39	**0:59**	**1:22**	**2:03**	**2:46**	**4:10**	**5:36**	**7:00**
	0:40	1:02	1:25	2:09	2:53	4:22	5:52	7:20
1:25	0:37	0:58	1:19	1:59	2:40	4:02	5:25	6:47
	0:39	**1:00**	**1:23**	**2:05**	**2:47**	**4:13**	**5:40**	**7:05**
	0:41	1:03	1:26	2:11	2:55	4:25	5:56	7:25
1:26	0:38	0:58	1:20	2:01	2:42	4:05	5:29	6:51
	0:39	**1:01**	**1:23**	**2:06**	**2:49**	**4:16**	**5:44**	**7:10**
	0:41	1:04	1:27	2:12	2:58	4:28	6:00	7:31
1:27	0:38	0:59	1:21	2:02	2:44	4:08	5:33	6:56
	0:40	**1:02**	**1:24**	**2:08**	**2:51**	**4:19**	**5:48**	**7:15**
	0:42	1:05	1:29	2:14	3:00	4:32	6:05	7:36
1:28	0:39	0:59	1:22	2:03	2:46	4:10	5:36	7:00
	0:40	**1:02**	**1:25**	**2:09**	**2:53**	**4:22**	**5:52**	**7:20**
	0:42	1:05	1:30	2:15	3:02	4:35	6:09	7:42
1:29	0:39	1:00	1:23	2:05	2:47	4:13	5:40	7:05
	0:41	**1:03**	**1:26**	**2:11**	**2:55**	**4:25**	**5:56**	**7:25**
	0:43	1:06	1:31	2:17	3:04	4:38	6:14	7:47
1:30	0:39	1:01	1:23	2:06	2:49	4:16	5:44	7:10
	0:41	**1:04**	**1:27**	**2:12**	**2:57**	**4:28**	**6:00**	**7:30**
	0:43	1:07	1:32	2:19	3:06	4:41	6:18	7:53
1:31	0:40	1:01	1:24	2:07	2:51	4:19	5:47	7:14
	0:42	**1:04**	**1:28**	**2:13**	**2:59**	**4:31**	**6:04**	**7:35**
	0:44	1:08	1:33	2:20	3:08	4:45	6:22	7:58
1:32	0:40	1:02	1:25	2:09	2:53	4:21	5:51	7:19
	0:42	**1:05**	**1:29**	**2:15**	**3:01**	**4:34**	**6:08**	**7:40**
	0:44	1:08	1:34	2:22	3:11	4:48	6:27	8:04
1:33	0:41	1:03	1:26	2:10	2:55	4:24	5:55	7:23
	0:43	**1:06**	**1:30**	**2:16**	**3:03**	**4:37**	**6:12**	**7:45**
	0:45	1:09	1:35	2:24	3:13	4:51	6:31	8:09
1:34	0:41	1:03	1:27	2:11	2:56	4:27	5:58	7:28
	0:43	**1:07**	**1:31**	**2:18**	**3:05**	**4:40**	**6:16**	**7:50**
	0:45	1:10	1:36	2:25	3:15	4:55	6:36	8:15
1:35	0:41	1:04	1:28	2:13	2:58	4:29	6:02	7:32
	0:44	**1:07**	**1:32**	**2:19**	**3:07**	**4:43**	**6:20**	**7:55**
	0:46	1:11	1:37	2:27	3:17	4:58	6:40	8:20
1:36	0:42	1:05	1:29	2:14	3:00	4:32	6:05	7:37
	0:44	**1:08**	**1:33**	**2:21**	**3:09**	**4:46**	**6:24**	**8:00**
	0:46	1:12	1:38	2:28	3:19	5:01	6:45	8:26
1:37	0:42	1:05	1:30	2:15	3:02	4:35	6:09	7:41
	0:44	**1:09**	**1:34**	**2:22**	**3:11**	**4:49**	**6:28**	**8:05**
	0:47	1:12	1:39	2:30	3:21	5:04	6:49	8:31
1:38	0:43	1:06	1:30	2:17	3:04	4:37	6:13	7:46
	0:45	**1:09**	**1:35**	**2:24**	**3:13**	**4:52**	**6:32**	**8:10**
	0:47	1:13	1:40	2:32	3:24	5:08	6:53	8:37
1:39	0:43	1:07	1:31	2:18	3:05	4:40	6:16	7:50
	0:45	**1:10**	**1:36**	**2:25**	**3:15**	**4:55**	**6:36**	**8:15**
	0:48	1:14	1:41	2:33	3:26	5:11	6:58	8:42
1:40	0:44	1:07	1:32	2:19	3:07	4:43	6:20	7:55
	0:46	**1:11**	**1:37**	**2:27**	**3:17**	**4:58**	**6:40**	**8:20**
	0:48	1:15	1:43	2:35	3:28	5:14	7:02	8:48
1:41	0:44	1:08	1:33	2:21	3:09	4:45	6:23	7:59
	0:46	**1:11**	**1:38**	**2:28**	**3:19**	**5:01**	**6:44**	**8:25**
	0:49	1:16	1:44	2:37	3:30	5:18	7:07	8:54
1:42	0:44	1:08	1:34	2:22	3:11	4:48	6:27	8:04
	0:47	**1:12**	**1:39**	**2:30**	**3:21**	**5:04**	**6:48**	**8:30**
	0:49	1:16	1:45	2:38	3:32	5:21	7:11	8:59
1:43	0:45	1:09	1:35	2:23	3:12	4:51	6:31	8:08
	0:47	**1:13**	**1:40**	**2:31**	**3:23**	**5:07**	**6:52**	**8:35**
	0:50	1:17	1:46	2:40	3:35	5:24	7:16	9:05
1:44	0:45	1:10	1:36	2:25	3:14	4:53	6:34	8:13
	0:48	**1:14**	**1:41**	**2:33**	**3:25**	**5:10**	**6:56**	**8:40**
	0:50	1:18	1:47	2:41	3:37	5:28	7:20	9:10
1:45	0:46	1:10	1:37	2:26	3:16	4:56	6:38	8:17
	0:48	**1:14**	**1:42**	**2:34**	**3:27**	**5:13**	**7:00**	**8:45**
	0:51	1:19	1:48	2:43	3:39	5:31	7:25	9:16
1:46	0:46	1:11	1:37	2:27	3:18	4:59	6:41	8:22
	0:49	**1:15**	**1:43**	**2:36**	**3:29**	**5:16**	**7:04**	**8:50**
	0:52	1:19	1:49	2:45	3:41	5:34	7:29	9:22

Table B.6 EN2-30 Seconds Rest

Repeat distance

Threshold	50	75	100	150	200	300	400	500
0:55	0:23	0:36	0:50	1:16	1:44	2:38	3:33	4:27
	0:24	**0:37**	**0:51**	**1:19**	**1:47**	**2:43**	**3:39**	**4:35**
	0:25	0:38	0:53	1:21	1:51	2:47	3:45	4:43
0:56	0:24	0:37	0:51	1:18	1:46	2:41	3:36	4:32
	0:24	**0:38**	**0:52**	**1:20**	**1:49**	**2:46**	**3:43**	**4:40**
	0:25	0:39	0:54	1:23	1:53	2:51	3:50	4:49
0:57	0:24	0:37	0:52	1:19	1:48	2:44	3:40	4:37
	0:25	**0:39**	**0:53**	**1:22**	**1:51**	**2:48**	**3:47**	**4:45**
	0:26	0:40	0:55	1:24	1:55	2:54	3:54	4:54
0:58	0:25	0:38	0:52	1:20	1:50	2:46	3:44	4:41
	0:25	**0:39**	**0:54**	**1:23**	**1:53**	**2:51**	**3:51**	**4:50**
	0:26	0:40	0:56	1:26	1:57	2:57	3:58	4:59
0:59	0:25	0:39	0:53	1:22	1:52	2:49	3:48	4:46
	0:26	**0:40**	**0:55**	**1:24**	**1:55**	**2:54**	**3:55**	**4:55**
	0:27	0:41	0:57	1:27	1:59	3:00	4:02	5:05
1:00	0:25	0:39	0:54	1:23	1:53	2:52	3:51	4:51
	0:26	**0:41**	**0:56**	**1:26**	**1:57**	**2:57**	**3:59**	**5:00**
	0:27	0:42	0:58	1:29	2:01	3:03	4:07	5:10
1:01	0:26	0:40	0:55	1:25	1:55	2:55	3:55	4:55
	0:27	**0:41**	**0:57**	**1:27**	**1:59**	**3:00**	**4:03**	**5:05**
	0:28	0:43	0:59	1:30	2:03	3:06	4:11	5:15
1:02	0:26	0:41	0:56	1:26	1:57	2:57	3:59	5:00
	0:27	**0:42**	**0:58**	**1:29**	**2:01**	**3:03**	**4:07**	**5:10**
	0:28	0:43	1:00	1:32	2:05	3:09	4:15	5:21
1:03	0:27	0:41	0:57	1:27	1:59	3:00	4:03	5:05
	0:28	**0:43**	**0:59**	**1:30**	**2:03**	**3:06**	**4:11**	**5:15**
	0:28	0:44	1:01	1:33	2:07	3:13	4:19	5:26
1:04	0:27	0:42	0:58	1:29	2:01	3:03	4:06	5:10
	0:28	**0:43**	**1:00**	**1:32**	**2:05**	**3:09**	**4:15**	**5:20**
	0:29	0:45	1:02	1:35	2:09	3:16	4:24	5:31
1:05	0:27	0:43	0:59	1:30	2:03	3:06	4:10	5:14
	0:28	**0:44**	**1:01**	**1:33**	**2:07**	**3:12**	**4:19**	**5:25**
	0:29	0:46	1:03	1:36	2:11	3:19	4:28	5:37
1:06	0:28	0:43	0:59	1:31	2:04	3:08	4:14	5:19
	0:29	**0:45**	**1:02**	**1:34**	**2:09**	**3:15**	**4:23**	**5:30**
	0:30	0:46	1:04	1:38	2:13	3:22	4:32	5:42
1:07	0:28	0:44	1:00	1:33	2:06	3:11	4:18	5:24
	0:29	**0:45**	**1:02**	**1:36**	**2:11**	**3:18**	**4:27**	**5:35**
	0:30	0:47	1:05	1:39	2:16	3:25	4:36	5:47
1:08	0:29	0:44	1:01	1:34	2:08	3:14	4:21	5:28
	0:30	**0:46**	**1:03**	**1:37**	**2:13**	**3:21**	**4:31**	**5:40**
	0:31	0:48	1:06	1:41	2:18	3:28	4:41	5:53
1:09	0:29	0:45	1:02	1:35	2:10	3:17	4:25	5:33
	0:30	**0:47**	**1:04**	**1:39**	**2:15**	**3:24**	**4:35**	**5:45**
	0:31	0:48	1:07	1:42	2:20	3:32	4:45	5:58
1:10	0:29	0:46	1:03	1:37	2:12	3:19	4:29	5:37
	0:31	**0:47**	**1:05**	**1:40**	**2:17**	**3:27**	**4:39**	**5:50**
	0:32	0:49	1:08	1:44	2:22	3:35	4:49	6:03
1:11	0:30	0:46	1:04	1:38	2:14	3:22	4:32	5:42
	0:31	**0:48**	**1:06**	**1:42**	**2:19**	**3:30**	**4:43**	**5:55**
	0:32	0:50	1:09	1:46	2:24	3:38	4:54	6:09
1:12	0:30	0:47	1:05	1:39	2:15	3:25	4:36	5:47
	0:31	**0:49**	**1:07**	**1:43**	**2:20**	**3:33**	**4:47**	**6:00**
	0:33	0:51	1:10	1:47	2:26	3:41	4:58	6:14
1:13	0:31	0:48	1:06	1:41	2:17	3:28	4:40	5:51
	0:32	**0:49**	**1:08**	**1:44**	**2:22**	**3:36**	**4:51**	**6:05**
	0:33	0:51	1:11	1:49	2:28	3:44	5:02	6:20
1:14	0:31	0:48	1:06	1:42	2:19	3:30	4:43	5:56
	0:32	**0:50**	**1:09**	**1:46**	**2:24**	**3:39**	**4:55**	**6:10**
	0:34	0:52	1:12	1:50	2:30	3:48	5:07	6:25
1:15	0:31	0:49	1:07	1:43	2:21	3:33	4:47	6:01
	0:33	**0:51**	**1:10**	**1:47**	**2:26**	**3:42**	**4:59**	**6:15**
	034	0:53	1:13	1:52	2:32	3:51	5:11	6:31
1:16	0:32	0:49	1:08	1:44	2:23	3:36	4:51	6:05
	0:33	**0:51**	**1:11**	**1:49**	**2:28**	**3:45**	**5:02**	**6:20**
	0:35	0:54	1:14	1:53	2:35	3:54	5:15	6:36
1:17	0:32	0:50	1:09	1:46	2:24	3:39	4:54	6:10
	0:34	**0:52**	**1:12**	**1:50**	**2:30**	**3:48**	**5:06**	**6:25**
	0:35	0:54	1:15	1:55	2:37	3:57	5:20	6:41
1:18	0:33	0:51	1:10	1:47	2:26	3:41	4:58	6:15
	0:34	**0:53**	**1:13**	**1:52**	**2:32**	**3:51**	**5:10**	**6:30**
	0:36	0:55	1:16	1:56	2:39	4:00	5:24	6:47
1:19	0:33	0:51	1:11	1:48	2:28	3:44	5:02	6:19
	0:34	**0:53**	**1:14**	**1:53**	**2:34**	**3:53**	**5:14**	**6:35**
	0:36	0:56	1:17	1:58	2:41	4:04	5:28	6:52
1:20	0:34	0:52	1:12	1:50	2:30	3:47	5:05	6:24
	0:35	**0:54**	**1:15**	**1:54**	**2:36**	**3:56**	**5:18**	**6:40**
	0:36	0:57	1:18	1:59	2:43	4:07	5:33	6:58
1:21	0:34	0:53	1:12	1:51	2:32	3:50	5:09	6:28
	0:35	**0:55**	**1:16**	**1:56**	**2:38**	**3:59**	**5:22**	**6:45**
	0:37	0:57	1:19	2:01	2:45	4:10	5:37	7:03
1:22	0:34	0:53	1:13	1:52	2:33	3:52	5:13	6:33
	0:36	**0:55**	**1:16**	**1:57**	**2:40**	**4:02**	**5:26**	**6:50**
	0:37	0:58	1:20	2:03	2:47	4:13	5:41	7:09
1:23	0:35	0:54	1:14	1:54	2:35	3:55	5:16	6:38
	0:36	**0:56**	**1:17**	**1:59**	**2:42**	**4:05**	**5:30**	**6:55**
	0:38	0:59	1:21	2:04	2:49	4:17	5:46	7:14
1:24	0:35	0:54	1:15	1:55	2:37	3:58	5:20	6:42
	0:37	**0:57**	**1:18**	**2:00**	**2:44**	**4:08**	**5:34**	**7:00**
	0:38	0:59	1:22	2:06	2:52	4:20	5:50	7:20
1:25	0:36	0:55	1:16	1:56	2:39	4:00	5:24	6:47
	0:37	**0:57**	**1:19**	**2:02**	**2:46**	**4:11**	**5:38**	**7:05**
	0:39	1:00	1:23	2:07	2:54	4:23	5:54	7:25
1:26	0:36	0:56	1:17	1:58	2:40	4:03	5:27	6:51
	0:38	**0:58**	**1:20**	**2:03**	**2:48**	**4:14**	**5:42**	**7:10**
	0:39	1:01	1:24	2:09	2:56	4:26	5:59	7:31
1:27	0:36	0:56	1:18	1:59	2:42	4:06	5:31	6:56
	0:38	**0:59**	**1:21**	**2:04**	**2:50**	**4:17**	**5:46**	**7:15**
	0:40	1:02	1:25	2:10	2:58	4:30	6:03	7:36
1:28	0:37	0:57	1:18	2:00	2:44	4:09	5:35	7:00
	0:38	**1:00**	**1:22**	**2:06**	**2:52**	**4:20**	**5:50**	**7:20**
	0:40	1:02	1:26	2:12	3:00	4:33	6:07	7:42
1:29	0:37	0:57	1:19	2:02	2:46	4:11	5:38	7:05
	0:39	**1:00**	**1:23**	**2:07**	**2:54**	**4:23**	**5:54**	**7:25**
	0:41	1:03	1:27	2:14	3:02	4:36	6:12	7:47
1:30	0:38	0:58	1:20	2:03	2:48	4:14	5:42	7:10
	0:39	**1:01**	**1:24**	**2:09**	**2:56**	**4:26**	**5:58**	**7:30**
	0:41	1:04	1:28	2:15	3:04	4:39	6:16	7:53
1:31	0:38	0:59	1:21	2:04	2:49	4:17	5:46	7:14
	0:40	**1:02**	**1:25**	**2:10**	**2:58**	**4:29**	**6:02**	**7:35**
	0:42	1:05	1:29	2:17	3:07	4:43	6:21	7:58
1:32	0:38	0:59	1:22	2:05	2:51	4:19	5:49	7:19
	0:40	**1:02**	**1:26**	**2:12**	**3:00**	**4:32**	**6:06**	**7:40**
	0:42	1:05	1:30	2:18	3:09	4:46	6:25	8:04
1:33	0:39	1:00	1:23	2:07	2:53	4:22	5:53	7:23
	0:41	**1:03**	**1:27**	**2:13**	**3:01**	**4:35**	**6:10**	**7:45**
	0:43	1:06	1:31	2:20	3:11	4:49	6:29	8:09
1:34	0:39	1:01	1:23	2:08	2:55	4:25	5:56	7:28
	0:41	**1:04**	**1:28**	**2:14**	**3:03**	**4:38**	**6:14**	**7:50**
	0:43	1:07	1:32	2:21	3:13	4:52	6:34	8:15
1:35	0:39	1:01	1:24	2:09	2:56	4:27	6:00	7:32
	0:41	**1:04**	**1:29**	**2:16**	**3:05**	**4:41**	**6:18**	**7:55**
	0:44	1:08	1:33	2:23	3:15	4:56	6:38	8:20
1:36	0:40	1:02	1:25	2:11	2:58	4:30	6:04	7:37
	0:42	**1:05**	**1:30**	**2:17**	**3:07**	**4:44**	**6:22**	**8:00**
	0:44	1:08	1:34	2:25	3:17	4:59	6:43	8:26
1:37	0:40	1:02	1:26	2:12	3:00	4:33	6:07	7:41
	0:42	**1:06**	**1:30**	**2:19**	**3:09**	**4:47**	**6:26**	**8:05**
	0:45	1:09	1:35	2:26	3:20	5:02	6:47	8:31
1:38	0:41	1:03	1:27	2:13	3:02	4:35	6:11	7:46
	0:43	**1:06**	**1:31**	**2:20**	**3:11**	**4:50**	**6:30**	**8:10**
	0:45	1:10	1:36	2:28	3:22	5:06	6:51	8:37
1:39	0:41	1:04	1:28	2:15	3:04	4:38	6:14	7:50
	0:43	**1:07**	**1:32**	**2:22**	**3:13**	**4:53**	**6:34**	**8:15**
	0:46	1:11	1:37	2:29	3:24	5:09	6:56	8:42
1:40	0:41	1:04	1:29	2:16	3:05	4:41	6:18	7:55
	0:44	**1:08**	**1:33**	**2:23**	**3:15**	**4:56**	**6:38**	**8:20**
	0:46	1:11	1:38	2:31	3:26	5:12	7:00	8:48
1:41	0:42	1:05	1:29	2:17	3:07	4:43	6:22	7:59
	0:44	**1:08**	**1:34**	**2:24**	**3:17**	**4:59**	**6:42**	**8:25**
	0:47	1:12	1:39	2:33	3:28	5:15	7:05	8:54
1:42	0:42	1:05	1:30	2:18	3:09	4:46	6:25	8:04
	0:45	**1:09**	**1:35**	**2:26**	**3:19**	**5:01**	**6:46**	**8:30**
	0:47	1:13	1:41	2:34	3:30	5:19	7:09	8:59
1:43	0:43	1:06	1:31	2:20	3:11	4:49	6:29	8:08
	0:45	**1:10**	**1:36**	**2:27**	**3:21**	**5:04**	**6:50**	**8:35**
	0:48	1:14	1:42	2:36	3:33	5:22	7:14	9:05
1:44	0:43	1:07	1:32	2:21	3:12	4:51	6:32	8:13
	0:45	**1:10**	**1:37**	**2:29**	**3:23**	**5:07**	**6:54**	**8:40**
	0:48	1:14	1:43	2:37	3:35	5:25	7:18	9:10
1:45	0:43	1:07	1:33	2:22	3:14	4:54	6:36	8:17
	0:46	**1:11**	**1:38**	**2:30**	**3:25**	**5:10**	**6:58**	**8:45**
	0:49	1:15	1:44	2:39	3:37	5:29	7:23	9:16
1:46	0:44	1:08	1:34	2:24	3:16	4:57	6:39	8:22
	0:46	**1:12**	**1:39**	**2:32**	**3:27**	**5:13**	**7:02**	**8:50**
	0:49	1:16	1:45	2:41	3:39	5:32	7:27	9:22

Table B.7 EN3-30 Seconds Rest (7%, 5%, and 3% faster than EN2-30 time)

Repeat distance

Threshold	50	75	100	150	200	300	400	500
0:55	0:22	0:35	0:48	1:14	1:40	2:32	3:25	4:17
	0:23	0:35	0:49	1:15	1:42	2:35	3:28	4:22
	0:23	0:36	0:50	1:16	1:44	2:38	3:33	4:27
0:56	0:23	0:35	0:49	1:15	1:42	2:35	3:28	4:22
	0:23	0:36	0:50	1:16	1:44	2:38	3:32	4:27
	0:24	0:37	0:51	1:18	1:46	2:41	3:36	4:32
0:57	0:23	0:36	0:50	1:16	1:44	2:37	3:32	4:26
	0:24	0:37	0:51	1:18	1:46	2:40	3:36	4:31
	0:24	0:37	0:52	1:19	1:48	2:44	3:40	4:37
0:58	0:24	0:37	0:51	1:18	1:46	2:40	3:36	4:31
	0:24	0:37	0:52	1:19	1:48	2:43	3:40	4:36
	0:25	0:38	0:53	1:21	1:50	2:46	3:44	4:42
0:59	0:24	0:37	0:51	1:19	1:48	2:43	3:39	4:36
	0:25	0:38	0:52	1:20	1:50	2:46	3:44	4:41
	0:25	0:39	0:53	1:22	1:52	2:49	3:48	4:46
1:00	0:24	0:38	0:52	1:20	1:49	2:46	3:43	4:40
	0:25	0:39	0:53	1:22	1:51	2:49	3:47	4:46
	0:25	0:39	0:54	1:23	1:54	2:52	3:52	4:51
1:01	0:25	0:39	0:53	1:22	1:51	2:49	3:47	4:45
	0:25	0:39	0:54	1:23	1:53	2:52	3:51	4:50
	0:26	0:40	0:55	1:25	1:56	2:55	3:56	4:56
1:02	0:25	0:39	0:54	1:23	1:53	2:51	3:51	4:50
	0:26	0:40	0:55	1:24	1:55	2:55	3:55	4:55
	0:26	0:41	0:56	1:26	1:57	2:58	4:00	5:01
1:03	0:26	0:40	0:55	1:24	1:55	2:54	3:54	4:54
	0:26	0:41	0:56	1:26	1:57	2:57	3:59	5:00
	0:27	0:41	0:57	1:27	1:59	3:01	4:03	5:06
1:04	0:26	0:40	0:56	1:26	1:57	2:57	3:58	4:59
	0:27	0:41	0:57	1:27	1:59	3:00	4:03	5:05
	0:27	0:42	0:58	1:29	2:01	3:04	4:07	5:11
1:05	0:27	0:41	0:57	1:27	1:59	3:00	4:02	5:04
	0:27	0:42	0:58	1:29	2:01	3:03	4:06	5:10
	0:28	0:43	0:59	1:30	2:03	3:07	4:11	5:16
1:06	0:27	0:42	0:58	1:28	2:00	3:02	4:06	5:08
	0:27	0:43	0:59	1:30	2:03	3:06	4:10	5:14
	0:28	0:43	1:00	1:32	2:05	3:09	4:15	5:20
1:07	0:27	0:42	0:58	1:30	2:02	3:05	4:09	5:13
	0:28	0:43	0:59	1:31	2:05	3:09	4:14	5:19
	0:28	0:44	1:01	1:33	2:07	3:12	4:19	5:25
1:08	0:28	0:43	0:59	1:31	2:04	3:08	4:13	5:18
	0:28	0:44	1:00	1:33	2:06	3:11	4:18	5:24
	0:29	0:45	1:02	1:34	2:09	3:15	4:23	5:30
1:09	0:28	0:44	1:00	1:32	2:06	3:11	4:17	5:22
	0:29	0:44	1:01	1:34	2:08	3:14	4:22	5:29
	0:29	0:45	1:02	1:36	2:11	3:18	4:27	5:35
1:10	0:29	0:44	1:01	1:34	2:08	3:13	4:20	5:27
	0:29	0:45	1:02	1:35	2:10	3:17	4:25	5:33
	0:30	0:46	1:03	1:37	2:13	3:21	4:30	5:40
1:11	0:29	0:45	1:02	1:35	2:09	3:16	4:24	5:32
	0:30	0:46	1:03	1:37	2:12	3:20	4:29	5:38
	0:30	0:47	1:04	1:39	2:15	3:24	4:34	5:45
1:12	0:29	0:46	1:03	1:36	2:11	3:19	4:28	5:36
	0:30	0:46	1:04	1:38	2:14	3:23	4:33	5:43
	0:31	0:47	1:05	1:40	2:16	3:27	4:38	5:50
1:13	0:30	0:46	1:04	1:38	2:13	3:22	4:32	5:41
	0:30	0:47	1:05	1:39	2:16	3:25	4:37	5:48
	0:31	0:48	1:06	1:41	2:18	3:29	4:42	5:54
1:14	0:30	0:47	1:04	1:39	2:15	3:24	4:35	5:46
	0:31	0:48	1:06	1:41	2:18	3:28	4:41	5:52
	0:31	0:49	1:07	1:43	2:20	3:32	4:46	5:59
1:15	0:31	0:47	1:05	1:40	2:17	3:27	4:39	5:50
	0:31	0:48	1:07	1:42	2:19	3:31	4:44	5:57
	032	0:49	1:08	1:44	2:22	3:35	4:50	6:04
1:16	0:31	0:48	1:06	1:42	2:19	3:30	4:43	5:55
	0:32	0:49	1:07	1:44	2:21	3:34	4:48	6:02
	0:32	0:50	1:09	1:46	2:24	3:38	4:54	6:09
1:17	0:31	0:49	1:07	1:43	2:20	3:33	4:46	6:00
	0:32	0:50	1:08	1:45	2:23	3:37	4:52	6:07
	0:33	0:51	1:10	1:47	2:26	3:41	4:58	6:14
1:18	0:32	0:49	1:08	1:44	2:22	3:35	4:50	6:04
	0:32	0:50	1:09	1:46	2:25	3:40	4:56	6:11
	0:33	0:51	1:11	1:48	2:28	3:44	5:01	6:19
1:19	0:32	0:50	1:09	1:46	2:24	3:38	4:54	6:09
	0:33	0:51	1:10	1:48	2:27	3:42	4:59	6:16
	0:33	0:52	1:12	1:50	2:30	3:47	5:05	6:23
1:20	0:33	0:51	1:10	1:47	2:26	3:41	4:58	6:14
	0:33	0:52	1:11	1:49	2:29	3:45	5:03	6:21
	0:34	0:53	1:12	1:51	2:32	3:50	5:09	6:28

Repeat distance

Threshold	50	75	100	150	200	300	400	500
1:21	0:33	0:51	1:11	1:48	2:28	3:44	5:01	6:19
	0:34	0:52	1:12	1:50	2:31	3:48	5:07	6:26
	0:34	0:53	1:13	1:52	2:33	3:52	5:13	6:33
1:22	0:33	0:52	1:11	1:50	2:30	3:47	5:05	6:23
	0:34	0:53	1:13	1:52	2:32	3:51	5:11	6:30
	0:35	0:54	1:14	1:54	2:35	3:55	5:17	6:38
1:23	0:34	0:52	1:12	1:51	2:31	3:49	5:09	6:28
	0:35	0:53	1:14	1:53	2:34	3:54	5:15	6:35
	0:35	0:55	1:15	1:55	2:37	3:58	5:21	6:43
1:24	0:34	0:53	1:13	1:52	2:33	3:52	5:12	6:33
	0:35	0:54	1:15	1:54	2:36	3:56	5:18	6:40
	0:36	0:55	1:16	1:57	2:39	4:01	5:25	6:48
1:25	0:35	0:54	1:14	1:54	2:35	3:55	5:16	6:37
	0:35	0:55	1:15	1:56	2:38	3:59	5:22	6:45
	0:36	0:56	1:17	1:58	2:41	4:04	5:28	6:53
1:26	0:35	0:54	1:15	1:55	2:37	3:58	5:20	6:42
	0:36	0:55	1:16	1:57	2:40	4:02	5:26	6:50
	0:36	0:56	1:18	1:59	2:43	4:07	5:32	6:57
1:27	0:36	0:55	1:16	1:56	2:39	4:00	5:24	6:47
	0:36	0:56	1:17	1:59	2:42	4:05	5:30	6:54
	0:37	0:57	1:19	2:01	2:45	4:10	5:36	7:02
1:28	0:36	0:56	1:17	1:58	2:40	4:03	5:27	6:51
	0:37	0:57	1:18	2:00	2:44	4:08	5:34	6:59
	0:37	0:58	1:20	2:02	2:47	4:13	5:40	7:07
1:29	0:36	0:56	1:18	1:59	2:42	4:06	5:31	6:56
	0:37	0:57	1:19	2:01	2:45	4:11	5:37	7:04
	0:38	0:58	1:21	2:04	2:49	4:15	5:44	7:12
1:30	0:37	0:57	1:18	2:00	2:44	4:09	5:35	7:01
	0:37	0:58	1:20	2:03	2:47	4:13	5:41	7:09
	0:38	0:59	1:21	2:05	2:50	4:18	5:48	7:17
1:31	0:37	0:58	1:19	2:02	2:46	4:11	5:38	7:05
	0:38	0:59	1:21	2:04	2:49	4:16	5:45	7:13
	0:39	1:00	1:22	2:06	2:52	4:21	5:52	7:22
1:32	0:38	0:58	1:20	2:03	2:48	4:14	5:42	7:10
	0:38	0:59	1:22	2:05	2:51	4:19	5:49	7:18
	0:39	1:00	1:23	2:08	2:54	4:24	5:56	7:27
1:33	0:38	0:59	1:21	2:04	2:50	4:17	5:46	7:15
	0:39	1:00	1:23	2:07	2:53	4:22	5:53	7:23
	0:39	1:01	1:24	2:09	2:56	4:27	5:59	7:31
1:34	0:38	0:59	1:22	2:06	2:51	4:20	5:50	7:19
	0:39	1:01	1:23	2:08	2:55	4:25	5:56	7:28
	0:40	1:02	1:25	2:11	2:58	4:30	6:03	7:36
1:35	0:39	1:00	1:23	2:07	2:56	4:22	5:53	7:24
	0:40	1:01	1:24	2:09	2:57	4:27	6:00	7:32
	0:40	1:02	1:26	2:12	3:00	4:33	6:07	7:41
1:36	0:39	1:01	1:24	2:08	2:55	4:25	5:57	7:29
	0:40	1:02	1:25	2:11	2:58	4:30	6:04	7:37
	0:41	1:03	1:27	2:13	3:02	4:35	6:11	7:46
1:37	0:40	1:01	1:25	2:10	2:57	4:28	6:01	7:33
	0:40	1:02	1:26	2:12	3:00	4:33	6:08	7:42
	0:41	1:04	1:28	2:15	3:04	4:38	6:15	7:51
1:38	0:40	1:02	1:25	2:11	2:59	4:31	6:05	7:38
	0:41	1:03	1:27	2:13	3:02	4:36	6:11	7:47
	0:42	1:04	1:29	2:16	3:06	4:41	6:19	7:56
1:39	0:40	1:03	1:26	2:12	3:01	4:33	6:08	7:43
	0:41	1:04	1:28	2:15	3:04	4:39	6:15	7:51
	0:42	1:05	1:30	2:17	3:08	4:44	6:23	8:01
1:40	0:41	1:03	1:27	2:14	3:02	4:36	6:12	7:47
	0:42	1:04	1:29	2:16	3:06	4:41	6:19	7:56
	0:42	1:06	1:31	2:19	3:09	4:47	6:26	8:05
1:41	0:41	1:04	1:28	2:15	3:04	4:39	6:16	7:52
	0:42	1:05	1:30	2:18	3:08	4:44	6:23	8:01
	0:43	1:06	1:31	2:20	3:11	4:50	6:30	8:10
1:42	0:42	1:04	1:29	2:16	3:06	4:42	6:19	7:57
	0:42	1:06	1:31	2:19	3:10	4:47	6:27	8:06
	0:43	1:07	1:32	2:22	3:13	4:53	6:34	8:15
1:43	0:42	1:05	1:30	2:18	3:08	4:45	6:23	8:01
	0:43	1:06	1:31	2:20	3:11	4:50	6:30	8:10
	0:44	1:08	1:33	2:23	3:15	4:56	6:38	8:20
1:44	0:42	1:06	1:31	2:19	3:10	4:47	6:27	8:06
	0:43	1:07	1:32	2:22	3:13	4:53	6:34	8:15
	0:44	1:08	1:34	2:24	3:17	4:58	6:42	8:25
1:45	0:43	1:06	1:31	2:20	3:11	4:50	6:31	8:11
	0:44	1:08	1:33	2:23	3:15	4:56	6:38	8:20
	0:45	1:09	1:35	2:26	3:19	5:01	6:46	8:30
1:46	0:43	1:07	1:32	2:22	3:13	4:53	6:34	8:15
	0:44	1:08	1:34	2:24	3:17	4:58	6:42	8:25
	0:45	1:10	1:36	2:27	3:21	5:04	6:50	8:35

Resource List

Madsen, O., and M. Lohberg. 1987, May/July. "The Lowdown on Lactates." *Swimming Technique* 24(1):21-26.

Maglischo, E.W. 1993. *Swimming Even Faster*. Palo Alto: Mayfield.

Sharp, R.L. 1993. "Prescribing and Evaluating Interval Training Sets in Swimming: A Proposed Model." *Journal of Swimming Research* 9:36-40.

Stegmann, H., and W. Kindermann. 1982. "Comparison of Prolonged Exercise Test at the Individual Anaerobic Threshold and the Fixed Anaerobic Threshold of 4mM Lactate." *International Journal of Sports Medicine* 3:105-10.

Weiss, M., N.E. Bouws, and H. Weicker. 1988. "Comparison Between the 30-Minute-Test and the 300 m Step-Test According to Simon in the Women's National Swimming Team." [Abstract] *International Journal of Sports Medicine* 9(5):379.